How to Buy
Real Estate

PROFITS AND PITFALLS

[Newman, Joseph]

How to Buy Real Estate

PROFITS AND PITFALLS

BOOKS by U.S.NEWS & WORLD REPORT

A division of U.S.News & World Report, Inc.

Washington, D.C. 1970

CONTENTS

LIST OF ILLUSTRATIONS

PART ONE

Investing in
Real Estate

Making Money in Real Estate

Real estate ranks today as the largest single category of investment in the United States.

One study a few years ago showed that real estate assets accounted for more than 86 percent of the total value of all the tangible assets in the country. They outstripped the total value of stocks and bonds.

President Franklin D. Roosevelt once summed up a few of the reasons why real estate has become such a popular form of investment. "Real estate cannot be lost or stolen, nor can it be carried away," he said. "Managed with reasonable care, it is about the safest investment in the world."

Real estate is permanent. It is tangible. You can see and inspect land. You can live in the dwellings affixed to land, or you can use them to produce income. And you know that the land will be there tomorrow, and the next day.

The late syndicated columnist Arthur Brisbane said: "Except in real estate ownership, time works against us. Time makes us old, time puts everything out of date, diminishes all values . . . except in real estate.

"The earth remains—it is man's property."

Brisbane touched on one of the powerful attractions of real estate. There is another. It offers a road to wealth.

Three wealthy Americans had this to say about real

estate as an investment:

Marshall Field: "Buying real estate is not only the best way, the quickest way, and the safest way, but the only way to become wealthy."

Andrew Carnegie: "Ninety percent of all millionaires became so through owning real estate. More money has been made in real estate than in all industrial investments combined. The wise young man or wage earner invests his money in real estate."

John D. Rockefeller: "The fortunes of the future will be made in real estate."

Field, Carnegie, and Rockefeller, of course, made their millions in an earlier era, when America was younger. Yet their comments are relevant in the America of today, and the America of tomorrow.

Loudoun County, Virginia, is an example of a modern-day real estate investor's dream.

Located a half hour's drive west of Washington, D.C., Loudoun County for decades was best known as the area where many prominent Washington families had country places nestled amid gently rolling hills.

But industrial and commercial development is bringing a new look to Loudoun County. The county's population is expected to quadruple in the seventies, and real estate prices already are reflecting the anticipated growth.

A 1,000-acre industrial tract shows in microcosm the rising land values in Loudoun County. The tract sold in 1949 for $125,000. Twenty years later it was sold again, this time to a major corporation. The price: $3 million. In two decades, the land's value increased twenty-four fold.

Big increases in value have come over shorter periods.

Recently, 100-acre tracts in Loudoun County were selling for $750 to $1,000 an acre. In 1964, owners thought they were lucky to get $500 an acre when they sold their property.

Another example:

An investor purchased 350 acres in 1960 for about $800 an acre. Ten years later, he sold 7 acres, zoned commercially, for $355,000, and another 17 acres for $68,000. He already has received $423,000 on an initial investment of $280,000—and he still has 326 acres to sell.

Smaller scale investors in Loudoun County real estate have done well, too. One purchased 77 acres in 1964 for $500 an acre, or a total price of $38,500. In 1969, he sold the property for $2,000 an acre, or a total price of $154,000. Another investor bought 84 acres nearby for $1,000 an acre and sold it five years later for a total of $269,000— or slightly over $3,200 an acre.

Even smaller parcels, selling in 1966 for about $750 an acre, were bringing $3,500 to $5,000 an acre in 1969. Generally, brokers say, the smaller the acreage, the higher the per-acre price.

Loudoun County is not an isolated example of dramatic increases in real estate values.

Not many years ago, when Walt Disney was assembling the land for his newest attraction in Florida, he paid an average of just under $200 an acre. Today, with the ambitious development emerging from the 27,400-acre site, similar land in the area is being sold for $5,000 to $10,000 an acre. One gasoline station chain paid $135,000 for a single acre of land adjacent to Disney World and fronting on a highway.

Across the continent, in California, real estate brokers tell of clients who have doubled their money in land investment in less than six months. Near Palmdale, California— 60 freeway miles north of Los Angeles—land prices increased from $15 an acre in 1950 to $8,000 an acre now, as industrial development sent the community's population soaring from 2,500 to 26,000 in two decades.

Among the most spectacular and widely known examples of rising land costs are those which have occurred along ocean frontage. A prime example is Ocean City, Maryland, which lies just north of the newly established Assateague Island National Seashore. Here is what happened to two lots:

Case 1: An unimproved block on the ocean, measuring 250 feet by 535 feet, in north Ocean City, Maryland.

Date of Sale	Price
1941	$ 3,000
1958	50,000
1965	225,000

THE BOOM IN LAND
(Market Value of all Taxable Land in the U.S.)

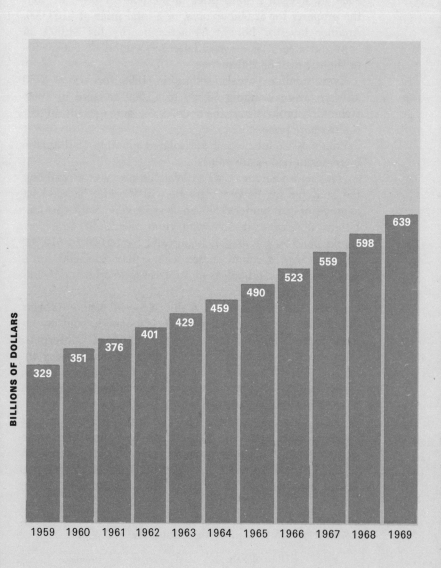

BILLIONS OF DOLLARS

1959	329
1960	351
1961	376
1962	401
1963	429
1964	459
1965	490
1966	523
1967	559
1968	598
1969	639

Source: USN&WR

Case 2: Another unimproved lot on the ocean, this one 50 feet by 142 feet.

Date of Sale	Price
1952	$14,500
1955	18,000
1964	30,000

When you read these cases of dramatic increases in real estate values, you may think, "If it has happened to other investors, then it will happen to me, too."

You should, however, bear in mind that real estate investment is a complex field. It is one that requires more than a normal amount of study. There are pitfalls to be avoided as well as profits to be gained by virtue of the fact that real estate values, in general, are on the upswing, just as they have been for years.

Why real estate values will grow

In the United States, we have about 2 billion acres of useable land. A century ago, about 30 million people shared these 2 billion acres. Today, about 204 million people share them. In the year 2000, according to population projections, 300 to 320 million people will be sharing these same 2 billion acres.

Spurred in large part by the laws of supply and demand, the value of America's land has increased approximately five-fold in the past fifty years. In 1920, economists estimate the total market value of real property at about $150 billion. Today, they put its value at about 1.6 trillion—or more than triple the combined assets of all the commercial banks in the country. Experts say the annual increase in land values compares favorably with the combined earnings of all U.S. corporations, or more than $36 billion a year.

Barring a massive breakdown of the economy, even the pessimists agree that most indicators point upward in the housing and real estate field. Housing starts are an example. Experts say the potential for the 1970s is about 2 million housing starts a year—fully 30 percent higher than the rate in the first half of the 1960s. Population trends also come into play. As more of the postwar babies reach marriageable age, the annual new-family-formation

HOW U.S. CITIES WILL EXPAND
BY YEAR 2000

	Total Land Area In Square Miles		Percent Increase
	2000	**1970**	
Los Angeles Basin	4,921	2,116	133%
New York, N.J., Conn.	4,662	2,803	66
Chicago-Milwaukee	2,853	1,495	91
San Francisco Bay	2,104	1,145	84
Detroit-Toledo	1,868	1,018	83
Washington-Baltimore	1,713	796	115
Dallas-Fort Worth	1,611	1,015	59
Houston-Galveston	1,530	714	114
Delaware Valley	1,491	916	63
Southeast Florida	1,486	564	163
Cuyahoga Valley, Ohio	1,278	750	70
Atlanta (with Marietta)	1,100	468	135
San Diego	1,063	380	180
Minneapolis-St. Paul	1,047	730	43
Total, 14 Largest Areas	**28,727**	**14,910**	**93%**

Source: Urban Land Institute, 1968

rate is expected to reach about 1,380,000. This compares with an annual average of just under 885,000 in the early 1960s and an annual rate of about 1,150,000 in the 1966-1970 period.

Such figures indicate that the momentum will continue —that real estate values will move steadily upward in the remaining decades of the twentieth century.

The key factor, of course, is that the growth in population will be applied to a fixed supply of land. Other factors come into play, such as inflation, new approaches to commuter transportation, urban redevelopment, and decentralization of industry and retail outlets.

Most of the population increase in the future—some experts predict 80 percent or more—is expected to occur in urban centers. And the bulk of this growth will come in the suburban areas ringing the central city. This, in turn, will spur the scattering of plants in areas away from the central city. And it will pave the way for new commercial ventures—shopping centers, for example.

Improving transportation systems and the increase in the nation's automobile population also promote the growth of real estate values. Motels, service stations, restaurants, and the like seem to spring up overnight along any newly opened stretch of express highway.

Studies show that freeways give a new mobility to workers, shoppers, and students. They permit them to travel twice as far, in the same amount of time, as they could on conventional highways. Merchants have learned that freeway bypasses have made local streets available for local shoppers. Industries have learned that good highways make it possible to move large plants into suburban and rural areas; employees have discovered that freeways mean they can get to their jobs more quickly and safely.

According to these studies, freeways have a favorable effect on the value of land near them. They usually bring a change in land use. What once was farm land is converted to residential, commercial, and industrial uses. This generally produces a high percentage increase in land values. A few examples:

—In Atlanta, Georgia, undeveloped land along a freeway sold for $1,200 to $1,400 an acre. Before the freeway was built, it was selling for $100 to $400 an acre.

—In Chicago, land along two new expressways increased in value from 2.3 to 5.8 times.

—Near Los Angeles, property values for land served by a new freeway increased in value from 12 to 243 percent. Industrial property that was selling for $7,800 an acre before the freeway was built sold for $25,000 an acre afterwards.

Highway construction often has still another effect. It results, in many cases, in the demolition of housing. Authorities predict that removals of existing housing—through highway and other projects, conversion to other uses, and destruction by disasters like fires and floods—will eliminate 720,000 dwelling units a year from the market in the early 1970s. This compares with a removal rate of about 585,000 units a year in the early 1960s.

The trend toward shorter work weeks and earlier retirement also stimulates the rise in real estate values. Golf courses, amusement parks, bowling alleys, and year-round resorts help Americans spend their leisure time; and more and more retirement communities are being built to accommodate the new breed of retired Americans.

The government and big corporations are involved, too.

The federal government, under its redevelopment programs, is seeking to revitalize run-down neighborhoods in cities by spurring new apartment and office buildings and retail shops.

Many corporations, meanwhile, are buying up land—even though they have no intention of using it immediately. This stockpiling of land by corporations is prompted by the realization that our land supply is limited. Two recent examples:

—A major Wall Street investment firm bought heavily in a recreational complex near Los Angeles. One reason was that the complex included 700 acres of valuable real estate.

—Another money management firm bought a major horse racing track in the Boston area. Included in the $12 million purchase were 2,000 acres of land. Forty-five acres of the land were not in productive use. This unused land was later appraised at $10 million, almost equal to the

HOW POPULATION IS EXPANDING
IN URBAN AND NON-URBAN AREAS

	Percent Increase 1965-1975	
	Metropolitan Areas	Nonmetropolitan Areas
U.S. Average	12.4%	7.7%
Regions:		
New England	7.5	9.2
Middle Atlantic	6.1	15.2
East North Central	7.9	5.4
West North Central	8.0	−1.4
South Atlantic	18.6	10.0
East South Central	9.5	4.9
West South Central	15.7	6.6
Mountain	24.9	10.4
Pacific	23.4	17.2

NOTE: A metropolitan area is one which has a central city of 50,000 or more residences and has outlying areas with another 50,000 residences.

Source: Bureau of Census, Department of Commerce

total purchase price. An official of the firm, asked why it bought the horse racing track, replied: "It's the land, not the horses. Land is the base, and it's a profitable base, too."

All these factors add up to the increasing development of real estate. This development consumes more and more land, in turn creates even higher values for the remaining and as yet undeveloped land.

With the exploding population, it would seem that the trend would be toward use of less and less land per person. But, surprisingly, the opposite is true in many areas. In the Los Angeles area, for example, one study during the 1960s disclosed that lot sizes had increased about 25 percent from the preceding decade. And the typical homeowner not only has his larger lot, but he also is likely to have a summer home on the beach, or a few acres in the mountains as a weekend retreat.

The rising cost of living—inflation, in other words—is reflected in other housing statistics. In 1950 the average price of a lot for a new home bought with a government-insured mortgage was just over $1,000. By 1969, it had increased to $4,300—more than a 300 percent increase. At the same time, the average selling price of a new house and lot went from about $9,780 to about $20,563.

None of these trends, projections or predictions, of course, spells automatic success for the real estate investor in the years ahead. They do underscore, however, that real estate is a growing and vibrant field with a high potential of success for the investor with the patience and determination to learn the fundamentals of the business.

Pros and cons of real estate investment

The advantages of investing in real estate might be summarized as:

—A generally favorable rate of return on equity in income-producing property, and a generally favorable chance of capital appreciation in well-selected land.

—Special features of the federal tax laws, which have extra advantages for investors in higher tax brackets.

—The benefits of "leverage" which you can gain when you buy property by paying only a portion of the total price with your own cash.

The disadvantages of real estate investments might be summarized as:

—A lack of "liquidity" in your investment.

—The steady rise of local property taxes.

—The immense amount of paperwork often involved in real estate purchases.

—Possible problems in managing apartments and other income-producing property.

—A lack of solid statistical data on which to base investment decisions.

—Carrying costs, interest rate on real estate loans, a minimum of 9 percent plus insurance costs.

Now let's look in more detail at the pros and cons of real estate investments.

A question asked very often is: "What rate of return can I expect from a real estate investment?" Unfortunately, there is no pat answer. On some other investments—such as municipal bonds—you are guaranteed a specified return on your money because the bonds' yield is set in advance.

Real estate investments are different, largely because there are no two parcels of property precisely alike anywhere in the world.

As one rule of thumb, authorities say a good investment in real estate likely will produce a 10 percent to 15 percent annual return on equity, less carrying costs. And for those interested in capital appreciation, they say that it is not uncommon for properly selected land to double in value over a given period.

Over the years, many studies have centered on what an investor in real estate can expect by way of a return on his money.

One study by a university professor, covering Los Angeles properties acquired in the post-World War II years, gave this breakdown on average annual net income as a percentage of the original purchase price:

Commercial	9.2 percent
Residential-commercial	10.9 percent
Residential	9.8 percent

Other surveys indicate that, in a typical large city, apartment, store, and office buildings in good locations will

Before . . . . *Wilshire Boulevard, main street of Los Angeles, and the surrounding area in the 1920s.*

After . . . . The same area, forty years later, after the population explosion and urbanization had done their work.

show yields of from 8 percent to 12 percent, while improved real estate under long-term lease to responsible firms will bring returns of from 6 percent to 9 percent of the equity invested.

Lloyd D. Hanford, Sr., past president of the Institute of Real Estate Management, offered these guidelines on comparative yields:

> Generally speaking investment real estate will produce 1½ more percentage points of income than other investments. As a general guide, prime real estate will earn approximately 1½ percent more than the prevailing interest rate in the prime mortgage money market. Where prime mortgages are at 5 percent, prime real estate will sell to yield 6½ percent to 7 percent.
> Secondary property will yield from 2 percent to 4 percent above the prime mortgage rate depending on location, physical condition, tenancy and lease terms. Marginal properties will yield from 5 percent upwards above the prime mortgage rate.
> The interpretation of prime, secondary and marginal are subject to individual assessment with easier identification as to examples of prime and marginal. A broad gray area of classification exists in determination of secondary properties and it is here that the expert Realtor can be of invaluable assistance to the investor. It is also in this area that the largest number of desirable investments will be found.[1]

One study published a few years ago compared the investment performance of common stocks with the realized yield of rental property. For the comparisons, researchers selected 20 FHA-financed apartment houses and seventy-six industrial stocks and examined them for a ten-year period (1952-1962). They found that the after-tax return on equity investment in real estate averaged 12.1 percent for the decade, or roughly twice that calculated for the randomly selected common stocks. After-tax rates of re-

---

1. Lloyd D. Hanford, Sr., *Investing in Real Estate* (Chicago: Institute of Real Estate Management, 1966), p. 22.

turn on total capital investment were closely similar, as shown in this table:

Apartment Houses vs. Common Stocks
After-Tax Rates of Return
1952-1962

	Apartment Houses	**Common Stocks**
Equity Capital	12.1%	5.7%
Total Capital	6.0%	5.7%

The researchers added that "returns on real estate investment and on common stock vary widely among individual properties or issues, emphasizing the importance of analysis of individual issues and properties."

They said further that "the superior investment returns for apartment house investment from 1952 to 1962 were due almost entirely to special real estate tax advantages." [2]

A more recent study showed market value of all real estate increased 81 percent from 1959-1969. Common stocks, by contrast, rose only 18 percent in the same period, in terms of the Dow-Jones industrial average.

The tax situation is of great interest to the potential real estate investor. In the eyes of many experts, depreciation allowances—when correctly applied—are one of the great advantages of real estate ownership. The depreciation allowance can be very valuable because it can permit the owner of real property to shelter all or part of his income so that he pays no current tax on it.

The government's tax collectors realize that buildings get older and eventually wear out. So the Internal Revenue Service permits owners to deduct tax-free a certain amount of money each year on the theory that the money eventually will go to replace the building.

There are several ways to figure depreciation. The simplest is the "straight-line" method, whereby the cost of the building is depreciated equally each year for the economic life of the structure. The IRS figures an apartment building's useful life at forty years, for instance, and an office building's useful life at forty-five years. Since land does not wear out, depreciation is not allowed on it. The

2. Paul F. Wendt and Sui N. Wong, "Investment Performance, Common Stocks vs. Apartment Houses," *Journal of Finance*, vol. 20, no. 4, December 1965, p. 644.

allowance applies only to buildings and improvements.

Suppose that you purchase an apartment building for $1,200,000 cash. The land is worth $200,000, the building itself $1,000,000. So the depreciation applies to the $1,000,-000 invested in the building. If the building had a remaining life of 25 years and you use the straight line method, you would be able to write off 4 percent a year—or $40,000—in each of the next 25 years. If the building showed you a return of $80,000 a year, you could offset half that amount with the depreciation allowance and pay income tax on only $40,000.

Another way of figuring depreciation is at an "accelerated rate." This generally allows you to take larger depreciation write-offs in the early years and smaller allowances in later years. In some cases, when accelerated methods are used, there will be more depreciation than cash flow. In that event, not only is the entire cash flow sheltered but the excess depreciation can be applied to shelter any other income the owner of the property may have. However, this generally does not happen for more than a few years, though.

Depreciations and other tax advantages are discussed in detail in chapter six. For the present, we might consider how "leverage" can profitably be used to an investor's advantage.

Leverage—what it can and cannot do

"Leverage" is a technical-sounding term that simply refers to the use of other people's money to help you buy a piece of property.

It is possible to get a larger portion of the purchase price financed in buying real estate than with most other kinds of investments. In the stock market, for example, buying on "margin" allows only limited leverage. When you buy common stocks on margin, you put up a percentage of the purchase price. Of late, the margin requirement has been 80 percent. This means that if you want to purchase $10,000 worth of stock, you would have to make a "down payment" of $8,000. While there is some leverage implied in such an arrangement, you can easily see that it would be much less than in real estate purchases where a smaller down payment is made.

The complete absence of leverage can be seen in this example:

Suppose you believe that the market in rare gems will show a dramatic appreciation within the next few years. You therefore buy a brilliant, flawless, unmounted ruby for $10,000, paying cash for it. You then put the ruby in a safe place and await the anticipated upswing in value. After five years, the stone doubles in value. You take it out of hiding and sell it for $20,000. You have made a clear $10,000, or 100 percent, profit. That is an impressive profit, but the fact remains that the principle of leverage has not worked in this transaction at all. You had $10,000 tied up in the ruby for five years.

We might now consider how leverage can work in a hypothetical real estate transaction.

Suppose you find a tract of land that you feel is sure to appreciate in value. The price is $10,000. You arrange for its purchase, but instead of putting up the entire $10,000, you are required to advance only $2,500 and assume a debt of $7,500. The land doubles in value in the next five years. You sell it for $20,000, or twice the price you contracted to pay for it. Unlike the case of the ruby, you have invested not $10,000 but only $2,500. Instead of doubling your money, you have quintupled it.

The table below explains the transaction, and shows what leverage can do *for* the investor:

	Before	After
Value	$10,000	$20,000
Debt	7,500	7,500
Equity	2,500	12,500

But you should keep in mind that if the property loses in value, the debt remains the same and the loss in value is taken out of the cash investment. Suppose, for example, your $10,000 property declines in value to, say, $7,500 instead of going up in value. Then the table would look like this:

	Before	After
Value	$10,000	$7,500
Debt	7,500	7,500
Equity	2,500	-0-

These tables indicate the following: The heavier the mortgage, the greater the percentage gain to the owner when the property rises in value but the greater the loss when the value goes down.

These examples are for land—property that produces no income. But leverage can work, too, for the investor who puts his money into income-producing property.

Take the example of Investor A who pays cash for a $100,000 apartment house. Suppose, after collecting rents and paying management expenses, he has an income of $11,000. That is a yield of 11 percent on his investment, with no leverage involved.

Now, take the same apartment house, but suppose that Investor B makes a 25 percent down payment on the property, or $25,000, and finances the balance with a $75,000 mortgage at 8 percent interest. Annual interest charges would amount to $6,000. Instead of having $11,000 income, Investor B would have $5,000. But this is 20 percent of his $25,000 initial investment—or nearly double, from a percentage standpoint, the 11 percent yield realized by Investor A who paid cash.

This table compares the two investments, and illustrates the advantages of leverage:

	Investor A (*Without* Leverage)		Investor B (*With* Leverage)	
Cost	$100,000	(cash)	$100,000	($25,000 cash, $75,000 mortgage)
Income	$ 11,000	(11 percent of full value)	$ 11,000	(11 percent of full value)
Interest	None		$ 6,000	(8 percent of $75,000 mortgage)
Yield	$ 11,000	(11 percent of cash investment of $100,000)	$ 5,000	(20 percent of cash investment of $25,000)

A note of caution should be attached to the use of leverage on income-producing property. Suppose that Investor B encountered a larger-than-expected vacancy rate during the second year and found that his income from the

apartment building was $7,000, instead of $11,000. This is
how the table would appear:

	Before	After
Income	$11,000	$7,000
Interest	6,000	6,000
Yield	5,000	1,000

As noted in this table, when income falls off, the interest
burden remains the same and the loss is taken out of the
yield to the owner.

Disadvantages of real estate investment

Lack of liquidity is probably the most-often cited disadvantage of investing in real estate. Simply put, the question is this: "How fast can I get my money out if I need
it badly?"

With a portfolio of blue chip common stocks, of course,
you usually can convert your holdings into ready cash in
a matter of minutes. But selling a piece of real estate can
be time consuming. And there is always a possibility that
a quick sale will cause you to take a financial loss. For
this reason, before investing in real estate, money management experts offer this advice: You should have enough
resources so that some emergency will not force you to
sell at a loss to the first buyer who comes along.

Even under the best of circumstances, sale of property
is likely to take a month to complete. Complicated deals
may take a year. First you must attract the buyer, then must
enter into negotiations, then work out an agreement. This is
followed by the paperwork involved in closing a deal—
mortgages, deeds, title searches and the like.

Federal tax laws can work to the advantage of the
real estate investor, as indicated in earlier reference to
depreciation allowances. But the local tax situation can
pose a disadvantage. Almost everywhere, local property
taxes have skyrocketed. And property owners often feel
they are at the mercy of the tax assessor. It's a complex,
frustrating matter to appeal what you think is an un-
realistic tax assessment on your property. Much paperwork can be involved, and the court machinery can be
ponderous and slow moving. It may take years before

your case is ruled upon. All the while, you must pay the full tax assessment, hope for a speedy judgment and a refund.

For many, the biggest drawback to real estate investment is not the lack of liquidity, or local taxes, or the paperwork. It is the prospect of becoming a landlord. It is one thing to recognize and seize upon a good piece of income-producing property. It is quite another thing to take on the role of landlord.

How, for example, do you soothe the sharp-tongued widow in apartment 103 who complains that her faucets drip at night—although they never seem to drip when you or the plumber go to check them?

Or how do you deal with the blonde in apartment 204 whose all-night parties have the rest of the building in an uproar?

Or, in the case of commercial property, what do you do about a tenant who quietly shifts his retail operation to a semi-manufacturing endeavor in violation of the lease, as well as the city's zoning laws?

Unless you have the personality and temperament to cope with such situations, you face two choices: Either avoid such investments, or find some way to reduce or eliminate such problems.

The latter can be accomplished by hiring a competent apartment manager, or by placing your properties in the hands of a real estate management firm. Doing this will ease the headaches that come with being a landlord. But it also will reduce the net income from your property, since you will have to pay for property management services.

There is still another drawback to real estate investment—the lack of solid statistical data on which to base a decision.

When you are considering an investment in the stock market, a quick call to your broker will bring you a detailed and factual report on most corporations. You can find out the corporation's gross revenues, its operating profit margin and percentages, its net income, its dividend payout, its price range on the market, and its average yield for as many years back as you care to investigate. You can also get expert advice on how the company may do in the months and years ahead.

But where can you turn for information on a particular real estate investment?

The seller is probably assuring you that it is a "dream deal." But where are the statistics to back up his claim?

If, for example, it is an apartment house, you need to know what the vacancy rate in the city is running. If it is high, say 20 to 30 percent, the purchase of rental property could be a financial mistake. But if it is low, say 5 percent, you might have a gold mine. For the second quarter 1969, the vacant rate was 5.1 percent for apartments. The home-owner vacancy rate was 0.9 percent. Both are the lowest rates in the 1960s.

Government agencies have a mass of information on housing trends. But the information often is too generalized to be of much help. For instance, it does you little good to know that nationally there is a shortage of two-bedroom apartments. In your particular city there may be an over-abundance of them. Similarly, it is of little help to know that nationally there is a severe overbuilding of four-bedroom, two-bath, colonial-style houses. In your city they may be in short supply.

Fortunately, most large cities have organizations like real estate boards or apartment owners' associations which might have statistical information on the local situation. This may be of some help, although sometimes their figures are outdated.

Still another point to remember:

Real estate usually requires comparatively large sums of money, as compared with other investments such as stocks, bonds or certificates of deposit.

Suppose, for instance, that you have $1,000 available for investment purposes. You might have to search for weeks to find any type of real estate available for that amount of money—or even one where that amount would serve as a down payment. In contrast, with a call to your broker you could within minutes buy $1,000 worth of common stock. Or, with a five-minute stop at a savings and loan association, you could buy a $1,000 certificate of deposit bearing 5¼ percent interest compounded quarterly.

These various considerations explain why real estate is a complex field, requiring more than a normal amount of study. As noted earlier, there are pitfalls and, for those who can avoid them, great profits.

Which Investment Is Best for You?

Every town, every city in America offers investment possibilities in real estate. Rural areas do, too. There are vacant fields and residential lots, industrial buildings and commercial sites, apartment buildings and single-family houses, office buildings and shopping centers, motels and mobile home parks—the list is almost endless.

Before you decide which investment is best for you, ask yourself this question:

Can you afford to invest in real estate?

Money management experts say a family can sensibly consider investing in real estate when it can answer "yes" to these three questions:

1. Does your family have an emergency fund to tide it through a financial crisis? According to one rule of thumb, a family should be able to live for six months without its usual source of income. Other authorities say a fund equivalent to three months' take-home pay may be adequate for emergencies.

2. Does your family have sufficient life insurance to provide security for the family in the event of the breadwinner's death? If you determine that your insurance program is adequate, be sure to review it periodically, making any necessary changes.

3. Does your family have money to invest in real estate which it will not need for at least several years? As noted earlier, you should be prepared to leave your real estate investment untouched long enough to gain the full benefits from it.

If you pass muster on these three points, then you might then consider ways to multiply your money through real estate investments.

But first, you might ponder another question:

Why are you investing?

Is it to make certain that the estate you leave your family is adequate?

Or is it to provide security when you retire twenty or thirty years from now?

Or is it to finance a child's college education 10 years in the future?

You may have one of these goals, or perhaps some other objective, or a combination of several goals. In any event, it is important to fix your goal firmly in mind. It will serve as your guide when you consider the type of real estate investment that will best suit your needs.

Just as it is important to fix your goals, it is wise to decide beforehand whether to undertake speculative real estate purchases, or those of a long-range investment nature. Any speculative purchase has some qualities of an investment and, conversely, every investment has some qualities of speculation in it.

Authorities say a speculative purchase generally has two basic characteristics: It involves high leverage, and it has the potential for fast turnover.

By high leverage, we mean purchases which require a minimum down payment and a maximum of time in which to pay off the balance. There is a big drawback to this type of investment—the tight money situation. Many lending institutions in recent years of tight money have tried to discourage high leverage deals by imposing stiffer requirements—a larger down payment, a shorter repayment period and higher interest charges. This means that if you plan to engage in real estate speculation with borrowed funds during periods of tight money, you may encounter difficulty in finding a lender who is willing to advance the money. And you should brace yourself for a high interest rate. If you fear that the property you have in mind may cope with a high interest rate and return a profit, then it may lose its appeal as a speculation.

Unimproved or raw land usually ranks at the top of the list of fast turnover prospects. The secret of profits here, real estate advisers say, does not lie simply in buying raw land and then selling it to someone else interested in buying raw land. Rather, it lies in buying raw land and then converting it to what is called "higher usage."

An example:

An investor—let us call him Ed Adams—purchased 80 acres of raw land about thirty miles from the heart of a large eastern city. He paid $1,000 an acre, or a total of $80,000. Three years later, Mr. Adams was able to interest a large industry in the land as the site for a new plant. The corporation purchased it for $3,000 an acre—or three times what he paid for it.

Other examples of converting raw land to a higher usage can be found on the outskirts of nearly every city. What is now a housing subdivision most likely was raw land a few years ago. What is now a major shopping center was, not long before, a tract of unimproved real estate.

Fast turnover can come, too, in land that is likely to change in usage as a result of new highway construction. An illustration:

On the fringes of a southern city, land was selling for $100 an acre before a freeway was built. Soon after the road was built, the land began selling for up to $1,400 an acre—a 14-fold increase due entirely to the fact that it was adjacent to the new highway.

Each parcel has its own characteristics, yet land can be divided into broad categories. They include raw unimproved land, farm land, residential acreage and lots, commercial tracts, industrial land, and recreational land.

As increasing population presses against a fixed supply, land should become more valuable, and it generally does. But much land will never feel the press of growing population in our lifetime, and it will be passed by. In addition, much land is over-priced today. This makes it essential for the investor to know how to judge land values and land uses, how to know when to buy and sell, and how to convert land into profit and income.

Instances of quick and profitable turnover are not as common as might be expected. Every example of brilliant success is offset by the dismal experience of some other investor whose hopes turned out to be unfounded. This is best underlined by the cliche that "an investor is a speculator who didn't sell his property quickly."

For this reason, many real estate counselors advise investors to follow a balanced approach. If you are interested in speculative purchases, they say it is a good idea to also have some longer term real estate investment.

And it is wise to keep a big chunk of your capital either in a cash savings account or in some other highly liquid form of investment. This provides a cushion you will need to ride out the rough periods in the economy. It also gives you the freedom to capitalize on investment opportunities that may come along suddenly and be gone unless you snap them up almost immediately. If you are interested in the more speculative type of real estate purchases, experts say you should keep a large reserve fund— perhaps a cushion of 50 percent of your capital. Naturally, you will be dipping into this reserve fund on occasion. But as soon as possible, you should replenish it, perhaps by liquidating some of your less promising holdings. If you are interested basically in longer-term real estate investments, a smaller reserve fund—perhaps 20 percent of your capital—might be sufficient.

What types of real estate constitute long term investments? Here are a few:

• Residential Property. Many investors are attracted to the possibility of buying residential property, fixing it up, and either selling it at a profit or renting it out as an income-producing investment. The attraction can be traced to several factors. First, since the investor probably owns his own home, he feels he already knows something about residential property. Second, the outlay of money is normally smaller than is required for many other real estate investments. Thus the risk of a large financial loss is less. Third, financing is often easier to obtain than on other property. And fourth, there seems to be an increasing demand for renovated residential housing.

• Office Buildings. An office building under long-term lease to top-rated tenants is often described as one of the most conservative forms of real estate investment. With proper maintenace and upkeep, the building will have a long—almost indefinite—life. And with the white collar work force increasing annually, there seems to be no end to the demand for new office space. Office buildings need not be huge skyscrapers. There is a growing number of small office buildings which cater to doctors, dentists, accountants, lawyers, and other professionals who often seek locations away from central business districts.

• Shopping Centers. Shopping centers represent the biggest post-war shift in commercial real estate. They also represent a field where the amateur is at a major disadvantage. Shopping centers are highly specialized in their composition and layout. Expert help is essential in their planning. While shopping centers may take longer to become profitable than other properties, such as office buildings, they can be immensely profitable as the volume of trade increases.

• Condominium and Cooperative Apartments. Both of these methods of selling "space" occupying the same land area have become increasingly popular in recent years. In a cooperative, each apartment dweller is really a stockholder in the cooperative corporation which owns the building and the land. In a condominium, the resident owns his own apartment—much like a home owner—and also owns a share of common areas, such as hallways. For the real estate investor, these two forms of apartment ownership are of great interest because they enable the builder or developer to sell the completed building to an assured market immediately after completing it.

"Togetherness" in investments

Investing in real estate need not be a lonely, unassisted task. There are ways to enjoy "togetherness"—through syndicates, real estate investment trusts and real estate corporations.

Until the years following World War II, real estate had been largely the domain of the individual investor or the limited partnership. The public, for years, had generally placed its money in more traditional types of investments, such as banks and savings and loan associations, or in stocks and bonds. But about two decades ago, significant changes in investment patterns began to emerge, and public investment in real estate became widespread. We might consider the major forms of "togetherness" in real estate investments.

Syndicates

Real estate syndicates are varied, but they generally have one basic characteristic: the pooling of money for the purpose of investment. Normally, the syndicate's funds are invested in one building, a block of buildings, or a single large project. For example, a syndicate might be formed to buy or build an apartment complex in a city. Or it might develop a winter resort area many miles from the city. While most syndicates, as noted, are concerned with only single properties, a few have become widely diversified in type of operation and investment.

Private syndicates range in size from four or five investors to groups of 25 or 30—or in some cases as many as 100. In the smaller syndicates, the participants might be close personal friends or business associates. In the larger ones, the investors may not even know one another. They likely are brought together by a professional real estate man, and they seldom have anything in common—except their joint investment. The main reason these large syndicates are considered private is because they involve no advertising or public search for participants.

The person who invests in a syndicate generally owns a fractional share of the total syndicate investment. He is not personally responsible beyond his own interest for the debts and liabilities of the syndicate. In other words, if an investor buys a 10 percent share in the syndicate, he is liable for 10 percent of the syndicate's debts, but no more.

This form of a syndicate offers a substantial tax advantage over a corporation: the absence of a double tax. Because it is treated as a conduit, the syndicate itself is not taxed. Instead, each "partner" picks up his share of the syndicate's income—or loss—and treats it as personal income. The money is taxed only once. In contrast, a corporation pays taxes on income as a corporation, and then its shareholders pay taxes on the money they receive in dividends. The money is taxed twice.

Because income tax deductions for depreciation, mortgage interest, and property taxes can be substantial, many syndicates enjoy a high rate of return. The popularity of this form of investment is illustrated by the fact that an estimated $10 billion were channeled into real estate in the decade of 1950-1960 through syndicates.

There are, however, some drawbacks. When the syndicate is doing well, the investor usually has little difficulty finding a buyer for his interest. An investor may run into difficulty, however, if he tries to sell his interest in bad times, when the syndicate is not doing well. A potential investor should make a careful investigation before putting his money into a syndicate. In a few cases, marginal properties have been syndicated at inflated values. And there have been instances of careless accounting and management practices by syndicate promoters.

Real estate corporations

The real estate corporation, like the syndicate, is in the business of buying, selling, and owning real estate. The risk of investing in a corporation generally is less than investing in a syndicate. But, as a general rule, the return is less, too.

A corporation is created by law and has an existence all its own. The shareholders are not responsible for any of the corporation's debts. But, with incorporation, the income from the business becomes subject to double taxation, as mentioned earlier. First, the profits of the corporation, are taxed. Then, dividends are taxed when they reach the hands of stockholders. This tax bite is overcome in part by the corporation's deductions for depreciation, real estate taxes, interest, and operating expenses.

Perhaps the greatest advantage of real estate corporations—as opposed to smaller syndicates—is the diversification of investments which is possible. As noted, most syndicates limit themselves to one building, or one project. A corporation can invest in ten, twenty or more properties

U.S. CORPORATIONS
ACTIVE IN LAND DEVELOPMENT

Aetna Life & Casualty
Aluminum Company of America
American Broadcasting Companies
American Standard, Incorporated
Bethlehem Steel Corporation
Boise Cascade Corporation
Castle & Cooke Incorporated
Celanese
Chrysler Corporation
Connecticut General Insurance
(Hartford)
Disney (Walt) Productions
Ford Motor Company
General Motors
Gulf & Western Industries

Hallmark Cards
Hunt Foods
International Telephone & Telegraph
John Hancock Mutual (Boston)
Metro-Goldwyn-Mayer
Norfolk & Western Railway
Penn Central Company
St. Regis Paper Comapny
Standard Oil Company of California
Union Pacific Railroad
U.S. Plywood-Champion Papers
U.S. Steel Corporation
Westinghouse Electric Corporation
Weyerhauser

of all types—apartment buildings, office buildings, and shopping centers, for example.

Another advantage of the corporation is liquidity. It usually is easy for investors to buy or sell shares in a real estate corporation, whereas an interest in a syndicate tends to be less liquid. The corporation's liquidity, however, can be hampered by a sharply declining real estate market. At such times, even normally liquid shares can be sold only at a loss. But this does not happen often.

Liquidity can be especially important if the investor suddenly needs cash for an emergency. And this liquidity is enhanced when the real estate corporation is fairly well known and its stock, like that of other major corporations, is traded on exchanges or in the open market. Usually, it can be sold easily at the prevailing quoted price. And since prices of real estate stock tend to move with general market trends, it offers an extra hedge against inflation.

Still another key feature of the corporation is that its shares normally can be valued more easily than an interest in a syndicate. This simplifies estate planning and execution. And because a corporation's shares are divided into relatively small units, $100 or $500 a share for instance, it is easier to give the shares as gifts.

Real estate investment trusts

The syndicate was the star of the 1950-1960 decade in the real estate investment field. Thanks to tax law amendments which went into effect in 1961, the real estate investment trust became the star of the 1960s. The purpose of the amendments enacted by Congress was to give the small investor in real estate the same advantages enjoyed by investors who buy shares in mutual funds. By pooling his funds with those of others, the investor could reduce the risk through diversification of investments, gain the benefit of experts in the field, and get into projects which were too big for him to undertake alone.

At the same time, the real estate investment trust (commonly known as REIT) can, if it meets certain standards, avoid double taxation since the only tax paid is on distributed income. This is an obvious advantage over corporations, which face double taxation. Thus, from a tax standpoint, a REIT has much the same tax advantage as a small syndicate. But it has one advantage over a small syndicate: it can readily invest in a number of properties, providing a diversification not usually available with a syndicate.

In clearing the way for REITs, Congress imposed some requirements. They include:

—To qualify for the tax advantages, a REIT must pay out at least 90 percent of its net income to its investors (known officially as beneficiaries).

—There must be at least 100 shareholders, and no more

than 50 percent of the outstanding shares can be owned by five or fewer persons. This restriction is designed to insure that every trust would have broad ownership, and could not be used as a personal holding company.

—At least 75 percent of the gross income must be from investments related to real estate, and no more than 25 percent of the total assets can be in investments other than real estate.

—It cannot directly manage any property it owns, and it cannot engage exclusively in land development or land sales. This is designed to make certain that the REIT will remain a basically passive income-type investment in which the small investor is less likely to become victimized by a sophisticated management group.

—It must have shares or certificates of ownership which can be freely transferred. In other words, shares or certificates of a REIT must be similar to shares in a corporation. This requirement stems from the intention that a REIT be publicly held.

Obviously, the law relating to REITs was written to appeal to the small investor. But the REIT has also become attractive to the large investor. This stems from a fact of life that is at the heart of much real estate investing: tax advantages are especially attractive to the investor in the high income brackets.

Much of the tax advantage can be traced to the depreciation allowance. As the building grows older, it wears out, and the Internal Revenue Service allows the owners to set aside a specified percentage of the building's worth. This money, which is tax free, in theory is to be used eventually to replace the building. But here is how one real estate expert says the depreciation allowance, in practice, can work to the advantage of an investor in a REIT:

A REIT purchases an office building for $1 million— $900,000 for the building and $100,000 for the land. The cash down payment is $400,000 and the $600,000 balance is secured by a 6 percent mortgage. Annual payments on the mortgage are $45,000, including principal and interest. The rental income is $100,000 a year, and the operating expenses, including insurance, repairs, real estate taxes and management, are $19,000.

Here is how the annual statement on the property looked:

Profit and Loss for Income Tax Purposes

Rent Income		$100,000
Expenses:		
Mortgage Interest	$ 36,000	
Depreciation (5%)	$ 45,000	
Operation Expenses	$ 19,000	
Total Expenses	$100,000	
Net Profit or Loss		—0—

So, according to this annual statement for tax purposes, the office building showed absolutely no profit. Thus it paid no taxes. But look at this same building's cash flow statement:

Cash Flow

Rent Income		$100,000
Cash Disbursements		
Mortgage (principal and interest)	$ 45,000	
Operating Expenses	$ 19,000	
Total Expenses	$ 64,000	
Balance for Distribution to Shareholders		$36,000

Thus, although the building showed no profit for tax purposes, it was still able to return to its owners a 9 percent return on a cash investment of $400,000.

There are, of course, some disadvantages in REITs. One of them, ironically, is found in the feature that is one of the investment trust's principal advantages: the requirement that it pay out to its shareholders 90 percent of its income each year. While this requirement tends to give investors an excellent return on their money, it also leaves REITs with little in retained earnings with which to make future investments.

A few REITs, set up hurriedly in the flurry of activity after passage of the amendments, encountered management difficulties. Some acquired real estate which looked good on paper failed to live up to projected economic performance. So the potential investor is well-advised to make an exhaustive study before committing his funds to such a group enterprise.

One of the advantages of real estate syndicates, corporations, and trusts is that they generally require little of the investor's time. There also are several other types of "trouble-free" real estate investments.

"Trouble-free" investments

One trouble-free way to invest in real estate is to loan your money to a property owner against the security of a mortgage on his home, apartment, or business building. Depending on the type of mortgage and the current economic situation, yields can range upward from 6 or 7 percent. And the amount needed to get into the mortgage buying business can be as low as $1,000. Here are two hypothetical cases to show how it can be done:

Case One: Mr. Businessman wanted to build an addition onto his small plant so he could expand his production line. He had only $10,000 of the estimated $40,000 cost, but he heard that Mr. Investor was interested in placing money in a good first mortgage. So Mr. Businessman and Mr. Investor made a deal: Mr. Investor will loan Mr. Businessman $30,000 and will take a first mortgage on the new building. The mortgage will run for twenty years at 7½ percent interest.

Case Two: Mr. Homeowner wanted to buy a new house, but he had only $5,000 of the required $6,000 down payment. His real estate agent suggested he get in touch with Mr. Investor, who had expressed interest in investing some money in good second mortgages. So Mr. Homeowner and Mr. Investor worked out this arrangement: Mr. Investor will loan Mr. Homeowner $1,000 as a second mortgage on his new house. The mortgage will run for five years at 8 percent interest.

The investor in these cases gets a good return on his money—and he need not spend much time watching after his investment.

Authorities say you should keep this rule in mind: Never put money into a mortgage on property that you do not want to own. If the borrower is not able to make his payments, you may have to take over the building by foreclosure. Then you become the owner.

There are two major disadvantages to investing in real

estate through mortgages. The first is that the entire annual income from the mortgage is taxable. No tax shelters or deductions are available. For an investor in the 50 percent tax bracket, this means that on an 8 percent mortgage he really is earning only 4 percent net after taxes. If, however, you are in a lower tax bracket—for example, if you are retired—the tax bite would not be as great. The second disadvantage is that the investor who buys mortgages has little protection against inflation. Suppose, for instance, that in 1950 you bought a twenty-year mortgage at 5 percent interest. You would by 1970 get your money back, plus interest, but the dollars would have less buying power in 1970 than they would have had in 1950.

Another relatively trouble-free real estate investment is known as the "leaseback." Here is how it works:

Suppose that XYZ company wants a $50,000 building to house its offices, but does not want to tie up its own money in constructing it. Mr. Investor agrees to put up the money and, in return, the company agrees to rent the building from him for a specified length of time, say twenty years. The company agrees further to pay him annually a sum which will allow him to pay all the operating expenses, taxes, mortgage principal and interest and also give him a specified return for his money, such as 8 percent.

The leaseback may have special appeal to the wealthy investor, since the building's operating expenses, taxes, and interest charges can be deducted in computing federal income taxes.

Hotels and motels

Besides the types of investments already discussed, there are a number of commercial activities which began and depend heavily on a real estate investment but which are highly specialized in their operation. An example is a motel. This is not generally considered a real estate investment in the same sense as, say, an office building. The motel business is a highly technical field in itself. But whether a motel succeeds or fails depends in large part on whether the original real estate investment—the selection of the site—was carefully thought out.

Hotels and motels have been a rapidly expanding field in the past two decades. In 1950, it was estimated there were 50,000 motels in the United States, representing a total investment of $4 billion. But fifteen years later, the estimated number had increased to 65,000 and the total investment had soared to $10 billion. This has given rise to fears that the market has been saturated, and that intense competition in some areas will drive some operators out of business. In some areas, for example, motels seem to be piled on top of motels. Everywhere you look there is a big, blinking neon sign "MOTEL." But fifty miles down the road the opposite might be true—there may not be enough motels to meet the demand of travelers. This contrast underscores the importance of carefully investigating the entire field, particularly the location of the motel.

Another important point: A motel or hotel is a business as well as—if not even more than—a real estate investment. It requires special training and management abilities. Nevertheless, the real estate investor might be interested for two reasons. First, a big part of the cost of a motel or hotel is represented by real estate, and a big part of any future profit on resale probably will be due to a rise in the value of the real estate. Second, a motel or hotel is a location-oriented business. Its success in drawing customers will be due in large part to its location.

Both hotels and motels are defined as establishments whose primary function is to provide overnight lodging to the general public. They are open twenty-four hours a day, provide the traveler with utilities, furniture and fixtures, maintain a switchboard and a reception and service desk, and provide maid service. Drawing a distinction between a hotel and motel is sometimes difficult, especially with advent of the "motor hotel." Generally, it is considered a motel when a guest is able to go directly from his automobile to his room, or vice versa, without passing through a lobby.

The motel and hotel business has become so sophisticated in recent years that experts say only a few individuals have the money and experience to strike out on their own as an independent innkeeper. Many say about the only way to get into the business is to obtain a franchise from a nationwide motel or hotel chain. One reason is that success in a motel operation depends, more and more, on the "referral system" which offers the traveler an opportunity to make free advance reservations at another motel in the same chain. This has become so important in the motel business that a large number of independent motels have joined together to provide the same service.

Just as the motel business has become more and more sophisticated, so has it become more and more expensive to enter. For example, one nationwide franchise chain estimates that a new motel today costs $15,000 to $17,000 a room, in addition to the land. In other words, few individual investors can afford to enter the business without enlisting partners or forming a corporation.

Mobile home parks

The house trailer, that slate-gray hump-ended box on wheels which provided temporary shelter for many of Americans during and just after World War II, has undergone dramatic changes in recent years.

The mobile home, as the house trailer is known today, has shed its lackluster appearance in favor of lustrous enamel hues that reflect more modern times. And also swiftly receding into the past is the image of the esthetically displeasing roadside trailer park.

With the change in image has come an increasing demand for mobile homes. One in every three families moving into a single family housing unit in 1969 moved into a mobile home. With 400,000 mobile units being constructed a year, the Census Bureau estimates that more than 6 million people are now living in mobile homes.

Geographically, the greatest growth in the mobile home market in recent years has been in the South, where half of all mobile homes are being shipped. Next comes the north central states, with 24 percent, and the West, with 16 percent. The leading state for mobile home parks is California, with 2,075, followed by Florida with 1,158. Other states with a significant number of parks include Washington, 518; Pennsylvania, 503; Ohio, 502; Arizona, 451; New York, 422; Michigan, 420; Oregon, 416; Illinois, 396; Texas, 379; and Indiana, 337.

The availability of homesites in many areas has not kept pace with the boom in mobile homes. As Curtis G. Fuller, publisher of Woodall's Mobile Home Directory said, "There's no place for new mobile homes to go. This is a very serious situation; we need new parks."

One reason for the shortage of mobile homesites is that zoning laws in many cities tend to keep mobile homes out of residential areas and relegate them to the less desirable, industrialized sections of a community. Mobile home dealers in Maryland and Virginia, for example, agree that homesites are so few in their areas that there are long waiting lists at most parks. As one put it: "We need a more enlightened attitude on the part of zoning officials, who still remember what happened after World War II when tin can trailer camps mushroomed over the landscape."

In states where more modern zoning laws are in effect—California, Florida and several southwestern states, for instance—the trailer camps of the post World War II-era have given way to well-planned mobile home parks. These often offer features similar to a suburban housing subdivision—nicely spaced lots, landscaping, and community recreation centers with swimming pools.

The growth in the number of mobile homes offers the real estate investor the potential for profit. However, development and operation of a mobile home park has become a sophisticated business. Mobile homeowners will seek out well-planned and attractive mobile home parks, but they will scorn the less modern parks with their mudholes and ramshackle appearance.

If interested in a mobile home park, the investor may be wise to make an early check of the community's zoning laws. As stated earlier, some cities have zoning laws which discourage establishment of mobile home parks. If you determine that zoning laws pose no problem, then you are ready to start a search for a suitable site.

The best site is one that is high enough and level enough to insure good drainage. Heavily wooded or rocky sites could pose problems in clearing, grading, and landscaping the site. Shopping, service, and recreational facilities should be within a reasonable distance.

How much land will you need?

By one guideline, a fifty-space park will require about 6 acres. This figure is based on the assumption that each space will contain about 1,500 square feet, or an area about 50 feet by 30 feet. This means your fifty spaces will occupy one-third of a 6 acre site. The rest will be taken up by roads, the administration building, recreation and play areas, and laundry facilities.

In planning a mobile home park, authorities say it is best to subdivide the site to suit the needs of three distinctive sets of tenants—permanent residents (one year or more); semi-permanent residents (one month to one year); and transient residents (less than one month). In this way, the more permanent residents will be able to develop social contacts and live with a minimum of disruption. And the area for transients can be located in a section of the park where their mobile homes can be set into place and removed with ease.

The ultimate cost of developing a mobile home park will be, by one rule of thumb, about four times the per-space cost of the undeveloped land. In other words, if you figure the land will cost about $500 per space, you can anticipate another $1,500 per space to cover such costs as playgrounds, landscaping, grading, sewers, water systems, streets, concrete foundations and patios, the office, laundry facilities, and architectural, engineering and legal fees. In this case, the total cost of developing a fifty-space park would be about $100,000.

Monthly space rents range anywhere from a low of $20 to as high as $200, with the average in the $50 to $75 range. If you assume a monthly rental of $60 and a 90 percent occupancy rate, then a fifty-space park will produce gross income of $32,400 on the rental spaces themselves. From that, of course, would have to be subtracted the manager's salary and other expenses such as taxes, insurance, maintenance and repairs.

Just as there is a shortage of mobile home parks in many sections of the country, so is there a shortage of spaces for the increasingly popular travel trailers and campers. A travel trailer is classified as a trailer under 29 feet in length which can be towed by the average car with little difficulty. A camper is a small housing unit, either self-propelled or mounted on the bed of a pickup truck.

As Americans become more vacation and travel minded, some investors have fared well by developing overnight camps for these travel trailers and campers. These parks generally are located near metropolitan centers or tourist attractions. While the mobile home developer usually allocates no more than eight spaces per acre, the operator of a travel trailer park can accommodate twenty to thirty of the smaller vehicles per acre.

The travel trailer park, of course, must still have roads, utility buildings and an office. But these can be less elaborate than such facilities in a mobile home park. A travel trailer park, however, needs clean restrooms and laundry facilities, as well as electrical outlets for the trailers and campers. Depending on location, the rate for space in a travel trailer park is anywhere from $1 to $5 per night.

Having surveyed the wide range of opportunities to the investor, we might next examine in more detail one of the prime areas of investment—land.

How to Buy Land

Will Rogers, the Oklahoma humorist, once offered his friends this bit of advice:

"Buy land—they ain't making any more of that stuff."

Land, as Rogers noted, is limited in quantity. And as the population increases and cities bulge at their seams, land values all across America are increasing.

This, of course, opens up countless investment opportunities. Raw land, farm land, vacant lots, recreational land and industrial land are all possibilities.

But, as must be emphasized repeatedly, there are pitfalls. Perhaps the most important one to guard against is the temptation to dive into a land boom which is unsupported by solid developments, such as a population increase produced by industrial expansion.

A land boom begins when speculators think people will need land. Often acting on no more than an unsubstantiated rumor, they buy and hold land in anticipation of future demands. Their activity causes land values to rise. Other speculators see the upswing in prices, and they hurry to get in. Trading soars and prices skyrocket without regard to true market values. Land is bought simply because someone is willing to buy at a higher price and he, in turn, hopes to resell at a profit.

Then, somewhere along the line, doubts begin appearing as to the land's ultimate use. Sales lag. Some speculators, realizing the peak of the boom has been reached, quickly unload. Others see this and panic. Everyone tries to sell at once, and the bottom falls out of the market. The result is a real estate collapse.

This is what happened in Florida in the mid-1920s, prior to the state's tremendous growth of the last four decades. Lots in a proposed Florida subdivision jumped in price from a few hundred dollars to $100,000 each within a short period. But they quickly skidded back down to a few hundred dollars when the bubble burst.

Large-scale land booms of this type are relatively rare today. But they are far from unknown. Much more common are local land booms, brought on by rumors of a new industry or government installation to be built near town.

The best way to avoid falling victim to a false land boom is to get hard-core facts. One should be wary of rumors, and think twice about moving into a boom area. On the other hand, don't automatically dismiss the possibility of participating in an attractive growth situation by assuming that, sooner or later, the bottom will fall out.

Potential investors also are advised to be alert to long-term bargains that may be available after land booms blow up. Examples of how this paid off can be found in cases of investors who picked up land at low prices in the years following the Florida boom. One illustration: a parcel of land with a 200-foot ocean frontage could be bought for little more than the taxes due; in 1950, it sold for $20,000, and a decade later, for $240,000.

Raw land

We might next consider some of the investment opportunities in "raw land."

Raw land is defined as any acreage which is not in use and for which no specific use has yet been determined. It is undeveloped, unzoned, and generally unloved. And it usually is surrounded by other land in the same category.

Of all real estate purchases, raw land often is rated as offering the greatest potential for profit. But one point should be stressed. Such purchases generally are specula-

RISING PRICE OF RAW LAND
IN WASHINGTON, D.C. AREA

(1920=100)

	1920	1930	1940	1945	1950	1955	1960	1965
Washington, D.C.	100	236	258	272	375	*	*	*
Montgomery County, Md.	100	130	100	137	202	267	604	1,159
Pr. George's County, Md.	100	141	137	169	264	482	794	1,398
Arlington County, Va.	100	206	221	195	294	1,214	6,320	602[1]
Fairfax County, Va.	100	143	121	203	373	664	790	1,657

*No raw land available
[1]Land difficult to develop
Source: Department of Agriculture

tive in nature. Basically, the buyer of a piece of raw land is gambling on a directional growth in the population or other factors that ultimately will make his land more valuable.

For the investor or the speculator with limited funds, raw land is attractive because it is likely to be cheaper than other kinds of real estate. Consequently, he may be able to get more leverage or potential gain with a given number of dollars by spreading his dollars over a lot of raw land than by concentrating it on a smaller amount of improved urban land or income-producing real estate.

The advantages of leverage were discussed in an earlier chapter. To illustrate how it is used in raw land purchases, we might take the case of an investor—say, Jim Smith—who buys 20 acres of land at $500 an acre, or a total of $10,000. If Mr. Smith makes a 20 percent down payment, his total cash outlay would be $2,000.

If the price of the land increases to $1,000 an acre, Mr. Smith could sell the 20 acres for $20,000. Thus, without additional investment, Mr. Smith has land worth ten times his cash outlay. He puts only $2,000 into the land and now he can sell it for $20,000.

Of course, if Mr. Smith sells the land, he must pay off the $8,000 balance he owes. But that still would leave him with $12,000. He would recover his $2,000 down payment and have a $10,000 profit. This represents a 500 percent profit on a 100 percent appreciation in the value of the land.

Obviously, there are risks involved in buying raw land and holding it for appreciation. But these are cushioned somewhat by several tax factors. First, in computing your federal income taxes, you can deduct the taxes, interest, and other carrying charges. And if the hoped-for appreciation in value fails to materialize, any loss may be made fully deductible for tax purposes.

Sometimes it is possible for the owner of raw land to sell off some of the property, enabling him to recover some money or make mortgage payments while retaining the balance of the land for future development or sale.

A word of caution: Often, the owner is tempted to sell off the best part of the acreage first. He might, for instance, receive an attractive, unsolicited offer for a portion of the land with good road frontage. But selling off the best part first can be an unsound business practice. It leaves you with the poorer parcels to be disposed of later. If possible, it generally is best to dispose of the poorer sections of your acreage first, and then wait for the development of these portions to further appreciate the value of the better land you retained.

The risks of raw land

Experts point out there are several risks in speculating in raw land. The primary ones, in brief, are:

—The cost of carrying the purchase may prove to be unacceptably burdensome.

—The land may have legal or physical defects which could impede its future development.

—The land already may have become overpriced through speculative transfers from one buyer to another, with each succeeding price reflecting an optimism that may not be justified.

By the cost of carrying the purchase, we mean the expenses of meeting mortgage and interest payments, property taxes and assessments. Carrying costs now run at about 11 percent. You should not speculate in raw land unless you have a source of income or a reserve which will handle the carrying charges over a period of years. And when you buy a piece of raw land, you should assume that you are going to have possession indefinitely. Hopefully, this will not be the case. But if you work on this assumption, you likely will avoid becoming burdened with short-term, high-interest financing.

Before you make a commitment to buy raw land, you should make certain that there are no physical characteristics which could handicap its future development. For instance, you should check the drainage, the water supply, the terrain, and other features. If there are any physical disadvantages, make certain that the price is low enough to allow for grading or whatever else is needed to overcome the problem.

Careful investigation should be made, too, of possible building and zoning restrictions, the method of tax assessment, the current tax rate, and the likelihood of future tax increases. You should also make sure that the property is not under a cloud of disputed ownership.

You should bear in mind that one of the major disadvantages of raw land is its lack of liquidity. If your financial situation changes suddenly and you need to get your money out of the land quickly, you are apt to find that it takes months to find a buyer.

In addition, experts say that you should never make raw land speculation your main and only operation. Remember that ownership of raw land is a losing proposition until the actual moment of resale. An investor in raw land must, therefore, be ready and able to maintain the property until a profit can be gained from sale. Otherwise, he could be forced to sell at a substantial loss. It is for such reasons that experts advise against placing more than one-fourth to one-third of your total real estate investment in raw land.

How much should you pay?

One of the toughest problems in buying raw land as an investment is determining the price you should pay. By all means, investigate to see whether the land has been the subject of previous speculative transactions. This can be done by looking up deeds at the county courthouse, or wherever they are filed. You might also check to see whether any of the adjacent land has changed hands in recent years. You can determine the selling price by counting the tax stamps on the deeds. Each $1.10 in stamps stands for $1,000 of the amount involved in the transaction. For instance, if $11 in revenue stamps are afixed to the deed, the price was $10,000. Revenue stamps will not be found on deeds sold in the past two years, as the federal tax on real estate was repealed in 1968.

An examination of deeds for surrounding property may fail to turn up any transactions which would help you measure the price you might expect to pay for the property you have under consideration. If this is the case, you may want to visit several real estate dealers in the area who specialize in raw land. Ask them for their opinions on what the acreage you are considering might be worth on today's market. This may give you an indication of whether the price at which you can buy the land is a bargain.

Experts often caution against basing purchase and sale decisions solely on the asking and selling prices of similar properties. Instead, they say, the decision should take into account the eventual use value. In other words, try to estimate the use of the property in the future, when that time is likely to be, and how much it may be worth for such use. This will help to arrive at a figure you can use to compare with current prices prevailing in the same area.

Another word of caution: Substantial price appreciation must be anticipated to justify purchase of raw land with resale in mind. This is because of the commissions and other expenses incurred in connection with real estate sales. For example, buying land at $500 an acre and selling it two years later for $600 an acre appears to be good appreciation. But remember that in those two years you will have made payments on the mortgage, for property taxes, and real estate commissions when you sell. The cost of holding property has become so high that it must double in value every seven years to warrant holding it.

What should you look for in raw land?

As far as physical characteristics are concerned, land that is high, dry, and flat generally commands a better price—and is a better buy—than land which is low, wet, or steeply sloped. The latter could require extensive grading, filling, or draining before it could be made usable.

Experts say it is wise to buy raw land with plenty of road frontage. This makes development easier, and it bolsters your chances of selling off enough land to get your money back while holding the rest of the land for future appreciation. For instance, a road frontage of 1,000 feet usually will permit two access roads to be cut into the property, permitting maximum utilization of the tract.

Another key factor is finding the right location. You should seek land in the path of a city's growth—either residential, industrial, or commercial, depending on the land's eventual use. You may have to wait five years, ten years, or in some cases even longer for the anticipated growth to materialize. But the wait is worthwhile if you can sell for a substantial gain. It is often difficult—at times impossible—to predict accurately the way a city will grow. But you should make the effort. Past real estate trends can offer clues to the future.

You might find it helpful to go to the public library or city hall and study maps of the city as it existed in years past, such as in 1900, 1910, 1920, 1930, 1940, 1950, and 1960. Examine these maps and you will get an idea of the city's past growth patterns. If the bulk of the development in the eastern part of the city has been industrial in nature, then you can assume this trend probably will continue in the future. In other words, if you buy land east of the city, it should be with an eye toward future industrial use, rather than residential use. Checkerboard utilization of land has become more of an exception than a rule.

Farmland

The foregoing rules and suggestions may be helpful if you are interested in raw land as an investment. Let us next look at another investment possibility—farmland.

The value of farmland in America has increased 169 percent since 1950. Today, the total market value of farm real estate exceeds $200 billion. An average acre is valued at about $185—an increase of $120 per acre from the $65 average in 1950.

No doubt because of such impressive statistics, more and more city folks are buying up farmland as an investment.

Agriculture Department surveys show that nonfarmers are the purchasers of nearly 40 percent of all farms sold in the nation. In some sections, like the northeastern states, 65 percent of farm transactions involve nonfarmers.

In reporting these statistics, the Agriculture Department observed:

> The increased buying and selling of farm and rural land by nonfarmers further points out the emerging "dual land market" in many parts of the country. One portion is the traditional farmland transfer for agricultural uses. The other portion involves transfer of rural land primarily for nonfarm uses.

And in commenting on the continuing upswing in prices, the Department said:

> Much open-country land in portions of the northeast, Appalachian, and Pacific regions, as well as land close to urban centers in other regions, is being purchased for nonfarm uses. Market values in these areas reflect anticipated nonfarm uses, which also influence value of land still being used for farming. However, for vast areas of the country, most transfers are for agricultural uses, and prices are determined chiefly by returns for such uses.

The "nonfarm uses" cited by the Agriculture Department are varied, but perhaps the biggest factor is the increasing population in urban centers. Population projections indicate our urban population will double within fifty years. In terms of land needs, the next three decades should see a doubling of land for urban development. Much of this future land, of course, will be today's farmland. And it stands to reason that in the course of the shift of land from farm to urban use, the potential for profit is there for those who own carefully selected parcels of farmland.

Many experts caution city residents against rushing out and buying a farm with the intention of becoming an active farmer. The reason for the warning is obvious. Farming has become a highly sophisticated, technical field which requires plenty of expertise and money—as well as patience and hard work. Simply put, today's farm is no place for a "greenhorn."

What approach should you follow, then, if you are interested in farmland as an investment?

Several avenues are open. The first, and most obvious one, is to buy an existing and operating farm—preferably one that is for sale under forced circumstances. A second avenue is to buy raw land which has the proper drainage and soil so it can be converted to a productive farm. A third is to seek out a rundown farm that has operated submarginally and spend the necessary money to improve it so that it will support crops.

These three approaches, of course, envision resale to a working farmer. A word of advice: Seek out the suggestions of an expert in the field, such as a broker who specializes in farm properties. This is a complex area of real estate investment, and specialized knowledge is a "must."

Still another approach is to buy and refurbish a farm with the idea of reselling it to a "gentleman farmer"— someone who is more interested in the prestige of owning a "country place" than he is in the productivity of the farm's soil. The "gentleman farmer," for instance, is apt to be influenced by the farm's proximity to the city, its overall appearance and other features—such as a lake stocked with fish or a wooded area where he can go hunting. There also are certain tax features which appeal to part-time farmers, considered in a later chapter.

As mentioned earlier, there is potential profit for the real estate investor or speculator who buys up farmland near an urban center and converts it to other uses. Residential subdivisions each year are consuming thousands of acres that once was farmland. There also has been a movement of industries from crowded cities to suburban or rural areas, where new plants can be built at lower costs. And there has been an increasing demand for recreational facilities, such as lakes and reservoirs, which are located in rural areas.

If you are considering buying farmland near an expanding city, you might apply the same basic rules cited in the discussion of raw land. Basically, it is best to try to locate land which will be in the path of the city's growth —either residential or industrial.

The value of the land varies widely from one farm to another, but looking at the national picture, the biggest increases in dollar value of farmland in the past decade have come in the South. In all southern states, except Texas, Virginia, and Tennessee, farm real estate values have more than doubled in the period 1958 to 1968. Smaller increases occurred in the mountain states, the Great Lakes area, and the corn belt states.

The average increase in the dollar value of farmland from 1959 to 1969 was 73 percent. During this decade, the states which showed an increase of more than 100 percent were:
    Georgia, 168.7; Arkansas, 160.6; Maryland, 158.9; Alabama, 127.8; Mississippi, 127.7; South Carolina, 124.1; Vermont, 118.7; Louisiana, 112.2; Missouri, 109.3; North Carolina, 108.9; Oklahoma, 106.3; Tennessee, 102.5; Wyoming, 100.0.

The states showing an increase of between 75 percent and 100 percent were:
    Delaware, 97.2; Connecticut, 93.4; Colorado, 93.2; Kentucky, 88.3; North Dakota, 85.4; Arizona, 83.9; Maine, 83.1; Michigan, 82.2; Texas, 81.8; Virginia, 77.5.

How does an investment in farmland in these and other states compare with other types of investments, such as common stocks?

Agriculture Department real estate analysts say that since 1950 the nation's farmland—including buildings—has produced an average yearly return of 8.8 percent a year. This includes a yearly return from the land's production of 3.5 percent, and a growth in value equal to a compound annual rate of 5.3 percent.

During the same period, the analysts say, the dividend-price ratio of 500 Standard & Poor's common stocks has averaged 3.5 percent a year—identical to the annual return from farmland production. But common stocks have increased in value at a rate of 10.3 percent a year, nearly double the rate for farmland.

The analysts, however, caution against basing an investment decision solely on such figures. They note:

> Annual total returns to common stock show much greater variation than those to farmland—primarily because of larger price movements. In five years during 1950-1967, stock prices declined, compared with one year for farm real estate. Annual stock price movements ranged from a 15 percent decline to a gain of 37 percent. In contrast, annual farmland price changes ranged from a 1 percent decline to a 12 percent gain.
>
> The greater fluctuation of stock prices increases the uncertainty of an investment in common stock. In addition, prices of individual stocks or groups of stocks are even more volatile than aggregate movements suggest. However, significant variation in returns to land and price movements also exist. As previously noted, returns to land may vary considerably depending on such factors as managerial ability of the operator, weather, and prices. Hence, determination of the most profitable form of investment cannot be based solely on an aggregate analysis such as this.

Figures cited in the comparison of farmland investments and common stocks did not take into account a key factor: leverage.

As is true of nearly all types of real estate, an investment in farmland may yield higher returns to equity capi-

HOW DIFFERENT STATES SHARED
IN BOOM OF FARMLAND PRICES

Dollar Value Per Acre

State & Region	1959	1969	10yr. % Change
United States	**$108**	**$187**	**73.1%**
Maine	71	130	83.1
New Hampshire	107	183	71.0
Vermont	75	164	118.7
Massachusetts	291	506	73.9
Rhode Island	459	665	44.9
Connecticut	394	762	93.4
New York	136	237	74.3
New Jersey	568	916	61.3
Pennsylvania	181	311	71.8
Delaware	218	430	97.2
Maryland	236	611	158.9
Northeast	**177**	**321**	**81.4**
Ohio	242	382	57.9
Indiana	245	420	71.4
Illinois	294	487	65.6
Iowa	239	389	62.8
Missouri	107	224	109.3
Corn Belt	**220**	**374**	**70.0**
Michigan	174	317	82.2
Wisconsin	128	209	64.6
Minnesota	146	218	49.3
Lake States	**147**	**235**	**59.9**
Virginia	138	245	77.5
West Virginia	89	112	25.8
North Carolina	158	330	108.9
Kentucky	120	226	88.3
Tennessee	118	239	102.5
Appalachian	**129**	**249**	**93.0**

State & Region	1959	1969	10yr. % Change
South Carolina	$112	$251	124.1%
Georgia	83	223	168.7
Florida	188	316	68.1
Alabama	79	180	127.8
Southeast	**112**	**242**	**116.1**
Mississippi	101	230	127.7
Arkansas	99	258	160.6
Louisiana	156	331	112.2
Delta States	**113**	**266**	**135.4**
Oklahoma	79	163	106.3
Texas	77	140	81.8
Southern Plains	**77**	**145**	**88.3**
North Dakota	48	89	85.4
South Dakota	49	78	59.2
Nebraska	86	145	68.6
Kansas	99	159	60.6
Northern Plains	**72**	**119**	**65.3**
Montana	31	53	71.0
Idaho	109	162	48.6
Wyoming	17	34	100.0
Colorado	44	85	93.2
New Mexico	24	41	70.8
Arizona	31	57	83.9
Utah	52	81	55.8
Nevada	32	43	34.4
Mountain	**35**	**61**	**74.3**
Washington	141	203	44.0
Oregon	93	142	52.7
California	308	544	76.6
Pacific	**210**	**349**	**66.2**

Source: Department of Agriculture

tal—in other words, your cash outlay—than a comparable investment in securities such as common stocks.

The reason, of course, is the relatively low equity required for real estate investment. Down payments on land purchases average 25 percent of the purchase price, and often will be even lower. In contrast, the margin requirements for common stock have been set at about 80 percent. You would have to put up $800 in cash to buy $1,000 worth of stock.

An Agriculture Department report said:

> . . . as long as return on total investment exceeds the cost of borrowing, the investor with limited equity in farm real estate can have "equity leverage." Correspondingly, his rate of return on equity may exceed returns to investments having larger equity requirements.

Vacant lots

So much for farmland as an investment. What are the investment opportunities in the city?

Vacant lots situated in or on the fringes of growing cities have shown a steady increase in value in the past two decades. These statistics give an idea of how money can be made by investing in well-located vacant lots:

In 1950, according to Federal Housing Administration studies, the price of an average finished lot was $1,035. Ten years later, in 1960, the price had more than doubled, increasing to $2,447. By 1965, the price had gone to $3,442. Then, in 1969, the average price stood at $4,300. This is more than four times what the typical lot cost in 1950—or an average annual increase in price of 7.8 percent.

The average size of a finished lot has increased, too, but not nearly as fast as the price. In 1950, according to a survey by the National Association of Home Builders, the typical residential lot contained 7,558 square feet. In 1960, this figure stood at 8,932 square feet; in 1965 it was 10,312 feet. Then, in 1968, the average lot had 11,281 square feet —or roughly one-fourth of an acre.

You should bear in mind that these statistics are for the average lot. While the typical vacant lot has been appreciating at 7.6 percent a year, you can still end up losing money if your lot is in a poor location. Remember, too, that patience is required for your investment in a vacant lot—like most other types of real estate. One real estate dealer compared a vacant lot with a growing boy.

You cannot expect a young boy to do a man's work—nor can you expect a new lot to bring you near the profit you might expect from a more mature lot.

Like a boy in college, your vacant lot can be a constant expense. Taxes and interest must be paid regularly. And just as the cost of a college education pays off when a young man strikes out on his own with a good job, so the expenses of your lot will pay off when you sell it at a handsome profit.

What should you look for in a vacant lot?

Assuming interest in a residential rather than in an industrial section, experts offer these suggestions:

—Try to buy in an area that falls within a city's growth pattern. For example, if most residential subdivisions are being built in the western part of a city, while little building is taking place in the eastern section, you should look for a lot in the western part.

—Try to buy a lot with easy access to a major traffic artery, such as a new expressway, or within a half mile of public transportation.

—Try to find a lot within walking distance of schools, and within easy driving distance of shopping, churches, and recreational facilities.

—It usually is best to buy a level lot, or one that slopes gently to the rear so that drainage is away from the house rather than toward it.

—Remember that if the lot is attractively wooded, without too many large trees where the house ultimately will stand, it may have special resale value.

—Avoid lots which are on heavily traveled streets, or that are near such nuisances as industrial plants or busy commercial areas.

And you should, of course, check building and zoning regulations, as well as the current tax rate and whether any special assessments are anticipated for streets or other improvements.

It was pointed out earlier that it takes patience to allow a vacant lot to blossom to its full value. It is not unusual, for instance, for an owner to hold a vacant lot five years or more before selling at a profit. But you should also use caution not to hang on to your lot too long. It is risky to work on the assumption that the lot will always continue to rise in value. Many investors carry their property so long that they find themselves in a stagnant market where they can sell only at a price much lower than they had been offered a few years earlier.

There's a right time to sell. Figuring out precisely when that "right time" comes, of course, is one of the difficulties of real estate investment. One veteran real estate dealer offers this simple advice: "Use your intuition." Chances are you will make the right decision.

Recreational land

Americans have more leisure time than ever before. They also have higher personal incomes. A combination of these factors has fueled a boom in all forms of recreational activities—and this, in turn, has fueled a boom in recreational land.

There are several ways an investor can cash in on the recreational boom. One is to buy raw land near a new lake or recreational area and convert the land into vacation homesites or other uses.

To illustrate the escalating prices for recreational land, we might refer to statistics prepared by the Department of Interior's Bureau of Outdoor Recreation.

The bureau studied the course of land prices in a 309-acre tract in the Ashley National Forest in Utah, now within the Flaming Gorge National Recreational Area. The bureau outlined this development:

April 1956—Congress authorized the Flaming Gorge Dam and Reservoir.

January 1958—The federal government appraised the 309 acres at $12,000, or an average of $39 an acre.

September 1959—The federal government purchased 195 acres at $8,450, or about $43 an acre. The remaining 114 acres were valued at $3,550, or $31 an acre.

November 1962—Construction of the dam was completed

A DECADE OF RISING PRICES
FOR DIFFERENT TYPES OF LAND

	Ten-Year Value Increase
New Home Sites FHA Insured	82%
Farmland	73
National Highway Land*	75
Lands of Dam Sites*	125
Recreation Land*	100
Industrial Park Land[1]	100

*Government purchases

[1] Minimum estimate by Urban Land Institute
Sources: FHA, Bureau of Public Roads, Tennessee Valley Authority,
Department of Agriculture, and Urban Land Institute

and the reservoir started filling.

December 1965—The State of Utah paid $13,187 for 14.2 acres of land, or an average price of about $929 an acre.

April 1966—The federal government appraised the remaining 99 acres at $42,500, or an average of about $429 an acre.

This land in Utah was purchased by the state and federal governments for public use. But similar escalation in prices has been documented on private land adjoining public recreational projects.

An illustration of this point can be found in a case study of 304 sales of land adjacent to the Pearl River Reservoir near Jackson, Mississippi. In the decade before the project was announced, land prices in the area had been increasing at a rate of 9 percent a year. This is what happened after the announcement:

First year: Land prices in the area increased 165 percent.
Second year: Prices increased 191 percent.
Third year: Prices increased 216 percent.
Fourth year: Prices increased 236 percent.
Fifth year: Prices increased 258 percent.

Another study by the U.S. Corps of Engineers found that land adjoining two federal reservoirs in Arkansas—the Dardanelle project and the Greers Ferry project—increased in value 800 percent between 1960 and 1965.

In commenting on this survey, the Bureau of Outdoor Recreation said:

> Corps of Engineers experience indicated that there is normally very little accelerated escalation of land prices within a Corps of Engineers project boundary. However, there are speculation and steep escalation in value of lands immediately outside the project boundary, as might be expected, since these are lands which front the reservoirs or have good access to them and offer good summer or vacation home sites and other water-based recreational opportunities.

These examples have obvious meaning for the real estate investor. If you are buying recreational land as an investment, the key to profit lies in anticipating developments, such as construction of a lake, and buying before the rush starts.

Besides converting raw land to vacation homesites and similar uses, there are other ways to cash in on the recreational land boom. An outdoor activity like golf gives the real estate investor a chance to convert undeveloped land to profitable use. Here's how it can be done:

Golf courses—By one estimate, there are more than 12 million golfers in the United States. Although golf courses dot the countryside near cities and towns, any spring and summer morning will find long lines of golfers waiting their turn at the first tee. Facilities have not kept pace with the increased interest in golf. Anyone familiar with the laws of supply and demand will realize that this means golf courses offer a prime investment possibility.

But a word of caution: It takes a lot of land, and it

is an expensive investment to maintain. Experts recommend 80 acres for a nine-hole course, and 160 acres for an eighteen-hole layout. And this land is not likely to come cheap because it must be within relatively easy commuting distance of potential customers. In addition to land costs, it generally will take anywhere from $15,000 to $50,000 to grade, landscape, and provide drainage and seeding for a nine-hole course. For eighteen-hole courses, these costs are apt to range from $45,000 to $80,000. And then there are maintenance expenses. As a general rule, it will cost from $2,000 to $3,000 a hole per year to maintain the greens and fairways in playable condition.

Even with the demand outstripping the supply, however, simple ownership of a golf course does not automatically insure financial success. This is a complex field. A high degree of professional help is required in the planning, construction, and management.

Miniature golf courses—A miniature golf course requires much less land than a regular golf course and may give the real estate investor a better return on his money. Basically, a miniature golf course consists of nine or, more frequently, eighteen putting surfaces. Various obstacles and hazards are placed between the tee and the cup to add interest and challenge to the game.

A typical eighteen-hole miniature golf course requires less than one-half acre of land, in contrast to the 160 acres recommended for its full-sized counterpart. Also, maintenance costs, capital outlay, and the costs of operation are smaller. The average eighteen-hole miniature golf course can be maintained by one person. An investor can design his own course, or he can buy a packaged course anywhere from $3,000 to $9,000.

A miniature golf course usually does its best business during the evening. Fees vary, of course. Most often they are about fifty cents per player. Operators say that in a good evening, the course can gross as much as $200. And for a year, they say, it is not unusual for a miniature golf course to have net earnings of $15,000.

Driving ranges—Driving ranges often are built and operated in conjunction with miniature golf courses. A driving range with thirty-five tees requires about 12 acres of land which has been seeded, rigged with outdoor lights, and spotted with yardage markers. Other than that, about all that is required is a small shelter which serves as the pro shop and equipment such as a mower and a machine to retrieve the balls. Also, at least two golf clubs are needed for each tee, plus thousands of golf balls. Profit potential generally is good, with some courses grossing as much as $30,000 a year, of which about $15,000 is profit.

Pitch-and-putt courses—These courses, also known as Par-3 courses, have appeared in increasing numbers as more and more Americans take up golf. Pitch-and-putt courses are just like regulation golf courses except all distances have been shortened so that the average golfer can complete a hole in three strokes. Generally, five acres is adequate for a nine-hole course. The smaller land costs, coupled with lower costs of construction, maintenance and operation, can add up to a profitable venture, although reliable income figures are not readily available for these types of courses.

Corporate land rush

While increased interest in such activities as golf is fueling a recreational land boom, forces at work within the economy are producing a corporate land rush that reaches into all sections of the country.

As the decade of the seventies began, many companies bought land for immediate expansion of factories, even though signs of a business slowdown were cropping up. Other corporations bought with an eye toward expansion, sometimes as distant as ten years from now. But a surprisingly large number purchased huge plots purely for speculation. As a result, prices of industrial land soared, and available tracts became scarce in many parts of the country.

Examples of rising prices are numerous. One real estate agent in California recalled showing a prospect a choice site that was selling for $2 a square foot, or $87,000 an acre. The man pondered for a few months before deciding to make the purchase. In those few months, the price rose 25 percent. Other salesmen referred to land which was selling for $1.25 a foot in 1969 and $2.50 a foot in 1970. In five years, they predict, the price could hit $10 a square foot.

Buying land for expansion, of course, has always been regarded as a necessary business expense. But buying land for speculation is considered a more risky corporate venture. If the land remains unused and vacant, the corporation receives no immediate return on its investment. And it must pay taxes annually. So unless the land appreciates in value, it would be a poor use of the company's money. But corporate officials are not worrying. They seem convinced that land prices will continue to rise.

When one large publishing firm bought 200 acres of land about 60 miles south of San Francisco, it frankly described the purchase as a long-term real estate investment. The price it paid was reported at about $5,000 an acre. Within five years, experts in the area say, the land should be worth twice that amount.

Companies often buy up land because they want to be sure they have plenty when they decide to expand or build new plants. One major company's policy is to buy two or three times as much land as it needs in the initial building phase of most facilities. In 1956, this company bought 20 acres for a warehouse, although only 10 acres were needed at that time. But a dozen years later, the land was completely in use and the company had to buy another three-fourths of an acre for a parking lot. The price of the original 20 acres was $20,000 an acre. The price of the three-quarters of an acre bought twelve years later was $76,000.

Although it had to pay a stiff price for the small parcel, this company was lucky in one respect: at least the land was available. In Stamford, Connecticut, a New York suburb where several major firms have built plants and offices in recent years, local real estate agents say there is virtually no available land left. The supply of industrial property is tight in other parts of the Northeast and in the Chicago, Los Angeles, and San Francisco areas. There is a more plentiful supply in the South and much of the Midwest, but real estate men say prices are rising there, too.

How can the individual investor cash in on this corporate land rush?

There are several possibilities, including:

—He can buy raw land which is suitably zoned and located for conversion to industrial uses. Of course, he will be speculating on the movement of industry into his area.

—He can put his money into an industrial park being developed by a syndicate, real estate corporation, or real estate investment trust.

—He can set out to develop his own industrial park. This approach may require much capital. For instance, one study showed that it cost nearly $10 million to develop a 1,000 acre industrial park. Of this, only about one-fourth went for the cost of the land itself.

If you are searching for land for possible industrial use, there are several factors to keep in mind. Transportation perhaps is the most important. It is essential that the site have ready access to a highway and, in some cases, to railroad transportation. If water transportation is available in the area, then this should be taken into account, too. And, with some types of industry, having a major airport nearby can be important. Besides the availability of transportation facilities, the presence of utilities—such as gas and electricity—can be of great importance. So can the availability of an adequate water supply. And, most experts say, level land is usually better suited as an industrial site than hilly terrain.

Authorities have words of caution for investors who are considering ways of cashing in on the corporate land rush: Dealing in industrial real estate can be a puzzling field full of pitfalls. Before investing your money, you would be wise to make a careful investigation and talk to experts, such as real estate agents who specialize in industrial properties.

Profits in
Commercial Property

Commercial real estate holds appeal for investors interested in income-producing property. Unlike most land investments, which yield no regular income, commercial property can generate a steady flow of cash. At the same time, the investor can build up an equity in commercial property which he can sell later if he so desires.

In addition to the income-producing and equity-building aspects, there are other advantages to investing in commercial property. The commercial tenant is likely to pay his rent on time and maintain the property. And he is not likely to move on short notice.

Commercial property comes in all sizes and types to fit a wide variety of needs. There are small one-story retail stores, and huge shopping centers sprawling over 100 acres. There are skyscraper office buildings in downtown areas, and small professional buildings in the suburbs. There are simple outdoor parking lots, and mammouth multi-level parking garages.

Let us examine some of the investment possibilities in commercial real estate.

Shopping centers

The explosive growth of suburban areas following World

War II, combined with the decline of central business districts, resulted in a boom in the construction of shopping centers. And the boom is far from over, experts in the industry say. They estimate that there are about 13,500 shopping centers in the United States, with about 1,000 new ones being built each year. Within a few years, the industry anticipates that half of all retail sales will be recorded in shipping centers.

A shopping center is a unique type of commercial property. Broadly defined, it is a multi-store merchandising operation on a site owned, developed, and managed by the shopping center developer, to whom the stores pay rent. There generally is a unified architectural design, and there are large parking areas, usually occupying three quarters of the entire site.

Shopping centers usually fall into one of three categories.

The neighborhood shopping center is the smallest. It consists of a dozen or so stores on a site of perhaps 10 acres. It serves a trading zone which includes 5,000 to 10,000 households. The main tenants are apt to be a supermarket and perhaps a drug store. Other tenants will be such service-type stores as barber shops, dry cleaners, hair dressers, and shoe repair shops.

In the middle category are community shopping centers. They serve a larger trading zone—usually 20,000 to 30,000 families or more—from a site in the 20- to 30-acre range. The chief store in these centers likely will be a small department or variety store. There also usually will be a supermarket, a drug store, and other stores such as a florist and a clothing establishment.

The regional shopping centers are the largest. In many ways resembling downtown shopping areas, these centers usually sprawl over 50 to 100 acres or more, including parking for thousands of cars. They serve a trading zone including as many as a quarter-million families. These centers sometimes have 75 to 100 stores and shops, the major tenants being large department stores.

It is not unusual for large regional shopping centers to cost $10 to $20 million to build. The huge sums of money required all but rule out the involvement of the individual investor acting alone. More often, regional shopping centers are developed by syndicates or real estate investment trusts, with financing supplied by big institutional investors such as insurance companies.

The neighborhood and community shopping centers are more within the reach of individual investors, although they, too, represent sizeable investments. In any event, the development of shopping centers has become a highly specialized field. You would be wise to consult professionals before you entertain the idea of entering the field.

After consulting them, if you still are interested in investing in a new shopping center, the next step would be to make feasibility studies. These cover such aspects as population and size of the trading area; income level and purchasing habits of families within the trading area; present and possible future competition from other shopping centers; and accessibility to the site.

Selection of a site is an all-important step. The location has much to do with the success of any shopping center. The larger, regional shopping centers usually are located on a site which is fed by a number of highways and major streets, since they draw upon shoppers from as far away as ten or twelve miles. In many areas, regional shopping centers have sprung up along major expressways and beltways in suburban areas.

The community center draws shoppers from as far as five to eight miles away, so it, too, usually is accessible from major highways. The smaller neighborhood centers generally are located on major streets. Since they also cater to "walk-in trade," they should be accessible to pedestrians as well as motorists. The neighborhood center is where shoppers go to buy food, pick up dry cleaning, have their shoes resoled or their hair cut. Studies show that shoppers do not like to drive more than six minutes to reach neighborhood centers.

As a general rule, neighborhood centers should not be located within one mile of each other, and regional or community shopping centers should be at least three miles apart. Otherwise, the centers will be in an overlapping competitive position.

How much land is needed to develop a shopping center? Studies produce this guideline: You will need 1 acre to provide 10,000 square feet of building space and 30,000 square feet of parking space. This means that if you are planning a neighborhood shopping center with 40,000 square feet of building space, you will need at least 4 acres. For a community shopping center with 150,000 square feet of building space, you will need about 15 acres; for a regional shopping center with 400,000 square feet of building space, about 40 acres.

It usually is a good idea to acquire more land than actually is needed for the shopping center. The extra land can be used later for expansion, or, if not needed for that purpose, used as the site for apartments or office buildings. Land costs vary widely. They can run as high as $40,000 an acre for prime locations.

It usually is best, experts say, to seek out a site which is relatively level. This saves on grading costs. However, some "split-level" shopping centers have been built on sloping sites. The split-level design makes it easier to provide loading docks and the like.

There is an endless variety of shopping center layouts. In the larger centers, there appears to be a trend toward having stores face inward, onto the pedestrian mall. Others are designed so stores have entrances on both the mall and on the exterior of the center. An architect with shopping center design experience can help select a layout which best suits your site.

You will need the architect's drawings in hand when you set out to arrange financing for the shopping center. You will also need to have a signed lease with at least one major tenant. In the case of a neighborhood center, this might be with a supermarket; in a community shopping center it might be a variety store; in a regional shopping center it might be a department store. With commitments from major tenants, also called "lead tenants," it will be much easier to get other tenants to sign up. Because the "lead tenants" are so essential to a shopping center's success, they often are given space at a rate 25 percent or so lower than other tenants pay. In other words, if the average minimum rate is $2 per square foot, the lead tenant might receive a rate of $1.50 per square foot.

A study several years ago showed that the national

average rental for a regional shopping center was $2 per square foot of gross leasable space. For community centers, the average figure was $1.70 per square foot. For neighborhood centers it was $1.75. This $1.70 to $2 range should be considered low, since, with inflation, higher maintenance costs, and higher taxes, minimum rents have gone up in recent years.

Under most shopping center leases, the tenant pays the minimum rent or an agreed-upon percentage of his sales volume, whichever is higher. Generally, a shopping center developer makes certain that the minimum rental will cover his fixed expenses. And the minimum rental is the figure the lender uses in deciding whether to finance the project. But, as a general rule, the shopping center developer makes his profits from the percentage agreements. The percentage rental rate varies for different types of stores. For example, a supermarket which has a low markup and fast turnover may pay 1 to 2 percent of its sales, while a jewelry store, with a lower volume, may pay anywhere from 6 to 10 percent of its gross sales.

Besides the rent specified in the lease, tenants generally share the costs of maintaining common areas, such as the mall and parking lot. Most leases also include an escalator clause stating that the tenant will pay a share of any increase in real estate taxes.

In the first few years after a shopping center opens, a developer may have to depend upon the minimum rental rates to pay his bills. But then, as sales volume of the center's stores increases, he is likely to find the percentage agreements coming into play, generating handsome profits for his investment.

If you are interested in buying an existing shopping center, either on an individual basis or through a syndicate or real estate trust, you should seek answers to a number of basic questions. Experts in the field have advanced this checklist as a valuable tool for potential investors:

1. Is the center well designed and attractive? Such centers attract good merchants, and good merchants attract customers.

2. What is the quality of the construction? Poorly constructed buildings require greater maintenance.

3. What is the length of the leases? Obviously, the longer the term of the leases, the more attractive the proposition becomes to a buyer.

4. Is the center properly leased with compatible groupings? In many cases, there are unnecessary duplications, such as two supermarkets or two variety stores in the same center.

5. What is the level of minimum rents? Is it high, low, or in between?

6. How good are the opportunities to increase income when present leases expire, either by securing new tenants or increasing the rents present tenants pay?

7. What has been the sales trend of the various merchants in the center over a period of years? Have sales been up, down, or have they fluctuated? These trends can be important since percentage leases are involved.

8. What is the competition in the trading area? How strong is existing competition? What is the outlook for new competition in the future?

9. Is the center in a growth area? Or is its growth exhausted and the only thing the buyer can look forward to is a holding action and dependence on local or national economic factors?

10. Does the center contain undeveloped land? To what extent could this be used to build additional stores to meet possible future competition?

11. What about parking—is it adequate?

12. What is the age of the mortgage? Does it have a reasonable prepayment clause?

13. To what extent do the merchants contribute to the maintenance of common areas, and on what basis?

14. Is the landlord insulated against tax increases, perhaps through clauses in the leases? Taxes are one of the largest single items of expense, and unless the owner is protected his cash flow can be reduced by tax increases.

Retail stores

Shopping centers, as noted, are becoming the home of more and more of the new retail stores. Yet there are situations where small retail stores outside shopping centers provide investment possibilities.

Not all retail stores are good investments. Far too many are two-story buildings which have a vacant second floor producing no income at all. Others are poorly located, off the beaten path or in areas so congested that shoppers can find no place to park their automobiles.

Finding a retail store that offers prime investment possibilities is no easy task. It will take time and patience. It also will require knowledge of local business patterns and wide experience in commercial properties. As an investor, you may have the money, time, and patience. But to get the knowledge and experience, you may be wise to seek out a real estate broker who specializes in commercial property. His advice may save you from stumbling into one of the many pitfalls which mark this area of real estate investment.

One question you are apt to face is this: Should you construct a new retail store building, or should you buy an existing building, perhaps one in need of renovation?

The answer obviously will hinge on your particular situation. Depending on construction costs in your area, a small retail store could cost from $10 to $14 a square foot to build. One survey in California found that it cost about $60,000 to construct a one-story retail store building with two stores of approximately 2,500-square feet each. This figures out to $12 a square foot, and does not include land costs, site improvements, or signs. To illustrate how building costs are increasing, this survey showed that the same retail store building would have cost $47,000 in 1960, or $9.40 per square foot.

If you are interested in buying an existing store building, you should consider hiring an appraiser to look over the property. Besides physical wear and tear, a building can suffer economic depreciation as a result of deterioration of the neighborhood. Almost all stores require a new front once every ten years. Modernizing the store front may cost several thousand dollars, but it could help attract better tenants. Occasionally an opportunity is provided by a property which, though superficially unattractive, is located in a sound business location. It should include adequate parking facilities.

No matter what you pay for a retail store building, its

value depends entirely on the rent it can earn. A property which can be rented for $8,000 a year is worth four times as much as one which can be rented for only $2,000. In many small towns, flat-rent leases are common for retail stores. For instance, a lease for an office supply store might be $150 a month for a period of five years. In larger cities, percentage leases—such as those used in shopping centers—are more common. The merchant pays as rent a percentage of his gross sales. This percentage differs according to a store's profit margin or markup. For instance, a supermarket which has a fast turnover and a low markup may pay 1 or 2 percent, while a florist, with a lower volume and higher markup, may pay anywhere from 8 percent to 10 percent. Percentage leases offer a hedge against inflation and allow the landlord to share directly in the tenant's success.

You should use care in selection of a tenant for your retail store property. Most brokers advise landlords to avoid renting to novices or amateurs. It is best, they say, for a prospective tenant to have had previous experience in his line of business with a good record of past management. The fact remains that, in the case of percentage leases, the rent you receive will depend on the success of your tenant.

Experts in the field also stress the importance of finding a store in the right location. The location often governs the rent you can charge, and thus governs the value of the property. Some inexperienced investors have lost heavily by purchasing retail store property in poor locations. By getting sound advice—and following it—you may avoid this pitfall.

Office buildings

There is a steady and strong demand for office space in most American cities today. The demand results from the new technological age and the men and machines needed to support it. Meeting the demand has brought handsome profits to many investors who put their money into office buildings.

For the small investor, there is an obvious drawback. Large office buildings are multi-million-dollar undertakings. For instance, one study shows that a 14-story office building with dimensions of 100 feet by 125 feet would cost $5,652,000 to build, excluding land costs. Because the cost is far beyond the reach of most individual investors, office buildings often are purchased or built by real estate syndicates. By pooling the funds of a number of investors, syndicates are able to swing larger deals.

If you are interested in investing in a syndicate which is seeking to buy an office building, you should make a personal investigation of the property, looking for answers to questions such as these:

Where is the building located? The best location, as a general rule, is near transportation, parking, service facilities, financial institutions, restaurants, stores, and shops. A building in a growing business district will almost automatically increase in value, especially if it is located on a prominent street. Buildings located in a declining business area generally should be avoided.

Who are the tenants? Nationally known firms with a top financial rating are, naturally, the best tenants. These well-known tenants are apt to attract other high quality tenants to the building. As a general rule, the fewer tenants the better. It is better to have a few tenants leasing entire floors than to have a large number of tenants leasing tiny offices.

What is the rate per square foot? You should check to see if it is higher or lower than in comparable office buildings in the same area. You also should inquire about the length of the leases. The ideal lease, of course, runs for a longer period, such as ten or fifteen years. But in many places, a lease term of three to five years has become common.

What is the building's physical condition? A well-maintained structure of good construction has an almost indefinite life. Central air conditioning is generally better than a large number of individual units, which could pose a service problem. And high-speed self-service elevators usually are preferable, mainly because they do away with the need for elevator operators and thus hold down payroll costs.

Before you make the investment, it is a good idea to

make certain that both an accountant and a commercial real estate agent of your choosing have examined the books carefully. They will be able to spot hidden expenses which may not be apparent to you.

These points generally apply to large office buildings in downtown areas. But you need not think only in terms of a huge downtown skyscraper when you consider the profit opportunities of office buildings.

Professional buildings

In fact, an increasing number of small office buildings are being constructed on the fringes of business districts and in suburban areas. These smaller buildings cater to business and professional men who are not particularly interested in a high-priced downtown location. Examples are doctors, dentists, lawyers, accountants, architects, real estate agents, and insurance men. There is a natural tendency for people with similar interests to locate in the same building. That is why many of these buildings become known as "The Lawyers' Building," "The Medical Building," and so on.

Often, these professional buildings are projects of small investors interested in finding a tax-sheltered method of accumulating capital for retirement and family security. For example, a lawyer generally does not have available to him the pension and profit-sharing plans which are extended to corporate executives. Nor does his law practice lend itself to sale at a profit like, say, a retail business operation. So the lawyer and other professional people often turn to such real estate investments as a way to build up capital values for future use.

Let us examine the hypothetical case of Henry Smith, an attorney who undertook to invest in a professional building:

Mr. Smith obtained lease commitments from a half-dozen other lawyers interested in offices in a professional building on the edge of a downtown area, yet near the county, state, and federal courts. His calculations showed he would need about 10,000 square feet of space. Contractors told him such a building would cost about $12 a square foot, or a total of about $120,000. He found a suitable site priced at $20,000, so he figured the building and land would cost approximately $140,000. In discussions with lenders he found he could obtain a mortgage for 75 percent of the total cost, or about $105,000. This left about $35,000 which he would need in cash.

Financing charges would be in the neighborhood of $8,400 a year, assuming an 8 percent mortgage. In addition, Mr. Smith's investigation showed that expenses, such as taxes, insurance, utilities, and the like, would be about $20,000 a year. So, figuring a rental rate of $4.50 per square foot, this is how Mr. Smith's calculations shaped up:

Rental Income		$45,000
Expenses:		
Mortgage	$ 8,400	
Taxes, insurance,		
utilities, etc.	$20,000	
Total expenses	$28,400	
Net Cash Return		$16,600

Thus, Mr. Smith could anticipate a net cash return of $15,000 on his cash investment of $35,000—or a net return of about 47½ percent.

A large portion of this $16,600 cash return would be sheltered from taxes, since depreciation allowances come into play. And through the years, besides realizing a nice annual income, Mr. Smith would be building up an equity which could be sold when he was ready to retire.

Some professional buildings are specially designed to suit particular tenants. A building catering to lawyers, for instance, might be designed to include a common law library. Or a building intended for doctors might have space for laboratory facilities.

Location, of course, is most important. Many doctors prefer suburban locations, perhaps near a major shopping center. Other professionals, such as lawyers and accountants, generally seek locations nearer the city's business district.

From an investment standpoint, a well-located professional building under lease to reliable tenants is most attractive. Professionals like doctors and lawyers usually are prompt in paying their rent and generally are reluctant to move their offices once they have become established in a location which is convenient for them.

At times there are investment opportunities in converting older residential buildings into a professional building. For example, in one large eastern city, several prestigious law firms located their offices in what once were large, stately residences on the edge of the downtown district. And in several southern cities, old mansions have been converted into dignified offices for professional tenants. An extra advantage here is that the spacious grounds offer ample parking space. However, renovation may require a zoning change, and one should be sure to check the zoning laws.

Parking lots and garages

America's automobile population has risen rapidly since the end of World War II. Then there were about 25 million automobiles registered in the United States. Now there are more than three times that number. All the while, the nation's cities are becoming more and more congested. So acute is the problem that many cities have moved to get cars off the streets by either prohibiting parking altogether or by imposing restrictions, like one-half hour or one-hour limits at parking meters.

These factors combined have meant a boom for owners of well-located parking lots or garages. And it has attracted the attention of real estate investors, who see profit potential in the ownership of parking facilities.

Before we look at the ways a real estate investor can put his money into such facilities, a few words of caution are in order.

First, this is a highly specialized field. Amateurs are at a distinct disadvantage. But with some study and investigation, an investor can become fairly conversant with the ins and outs of the business.

Second, an investor faces possible competition from the cities themselves. As congestion worsens, a number of cities have built, with tax or bond funds, municipal parking facilities in their downtown areas. Since the city governments can command the use of tax-free land, and can obtain tremendous financing at reasonable terms, the rates charged at municipally owned parking facilities can be much lower than those charged by private lots and garages.

There are two basic types of parking facilities. One is the street-level lot. The other is the multi-story parking garage.

An investor can get into the business in several ways. He can own the facility and operate it, too. Or he can lease the lot to an operator under an arrangement that would give him, as owner, a percentage of the lot's income. Or he can own the lot, yet operate it under a management contract, paying the operator a percentage fee.

For the small investor, the simplest and least expensive facility is an outdoor lot where space is rented on a monthly basis. These lots generally can be unattended. The monthly renters park and lock their own cars. There are two drawbacks to unattended lots. First, there is a problem with freeloaders—people who try to use the lot without paying. And second, people who park their own cars are understandably wary about getting too close to other cars. Thus, you do not get maximum use of your lot space. Studies show that, with an attendant doing the parking, you can figure about 200 to 250 square feet will be required per car. With a self-service lot, you should figure 300 to 350 square feet per car. Both figures include the aisles. Put another way, a 10,000-square foot lot with an attendant can accommodate about fifty cars. Without an attendant, it will take about thirty-five cars. A single attendant can handle a lot with a capacity of between seventy-five and ninety cars.

An increasing number of multi-story parking facilities are going up in highly congested business districts. The reason for their growth is obvious. They make maximum use of expensive land. For instance, a seven-story parking facility built on a 20,000-square foot plot can accommodate about 700 cars. These facilities, which have ramps connecting the levels, can be either attended or unattended. Once again, if you let motorists do their own parking, you will not be able to fit in as many cars.

What will a parking facility cost?

For an outdoor lot, the cost of improvements—paving, fencing, painting, and signs—will run about $1 per square foot. This is in addition to land costs. The 10,000-square foot lot is generally considered the smallest feasible outdoor facility.

The multi-story parking garage will cost, in addition to the land, anywhere from $1,500 to $2,500 per stall. In other words, a facility with a 500-car capacity could cost from $750,000 to $1,250,000—plus land cost.

Selecting the right location is perhaps the key factor to success in the parking lot business. Generally, it is best to stay as close as possible to the business district. Land costs there will be higher than on the fringes of the business district, but the driver who pays for a parking space usually wants to be as close as possible to his destination. In addition, experts say the best site is near a "traffic generator," such as an office building, department store or large hotel. Keep in mind that an office building probably will generate most of its traffic during the day. The same is true of a department store, although some evening parking can be anticipated if the store has evening hours. A hotel is one of the best traffic generators since both day and night use can be expected.

Where feasible, it is helpful to have some sort of tie-in arrangement with nearby business firms. Under a typical arrangement, a department store offers customers a half-hour's free parking at a nearby lot. The store pays the parking lot operator a negotiated fee. It is somewhat less than his regular rate, but the operator gets the advantage of a higher volume of business.

The Apartment Boom

The typical young couple setting up housekeeping today is going into an apartment. So are many older couples whose children are grown and gone.

For most low income families, home ownership is all but out of the question. And, as costs continue to rise, many a moderate income family finds its chances of buying a house someday growing increasingly dim, unless the wife takes a job.

But for millions of people, apartment living is no hardship. They prefer it. They are moving into high-rise complexes or clusters of garden apartments, and are pleased. These families are bucking what, for generations, has been held out as the American ideal. From colonial times, homeownership has been regarded as a political, psychological, and financial advantage. What has happened to this goal?

Simply this: The cost of buying a house has risen beyond the financial capacity of the great majority of families.

One housing expert puts it this way:

The rapid increase in costs means that it is less and less possible for a family to buy a house if only one member is working. We are moving into an era of substantial housing shortages, and the basic makeup of family living is being challenged by increased costs.

The rising costs of single-family homes result from a combination of factors. Since 1950, land costs have gone up 7.8 percent per year on the average, or nearly 315 percent altogether. Cost of financing residential construction more than doubled between 1966 and 1970. In that period, the average mortgage interest rate to the home buyer rose from 6 percent to 8½ percent. Real estate taxes have gone up about 50 percent since 1963. Wage rates in building trades increased 22 percent from 1964 to 1968, while cost of building materials went up 11.5 percent.

All these factors have forced the prices of new homes up and up. The median price of new houses sold in the United States in 1969 exceeded $26,000. And in many big cities and suburbs, the $20,000 house is a rarity. Even the $30,000-and-under house is disappearing. "People are being priced out of the home ownership market," says one industry official. "Ten years from now a house under $40,000 will be a rarity. This is going to really fire up the multifamily concept."

Even in suburban areas, elevator apartments are springing up, generally close to major shopping centers or good public transportation. In the San Francisco Bay area, for example, suburban towns are encouraging high-rise apartment developments along the route of the Bay Area Rapid Transit line.

Actually, the trend toward apartments has been developing for years. In the early 1950s, multifamily units made up less than 10 percent of the nation's housing starts. The proportion has increased steadily until it now exceeds 40 percent. Reasons for this trend, aside from the high cost of buying a home, include:

—A growing scarcity of land close to cities where a majority of American families now lives. High-density development becomes more essential as the major metropolitan areas grow even larger.

—A transient population. One developer says, "These employes who are being shifted about all the time don't

MORE APARTMENTS
FEWER ONE-FAMILY HOMES

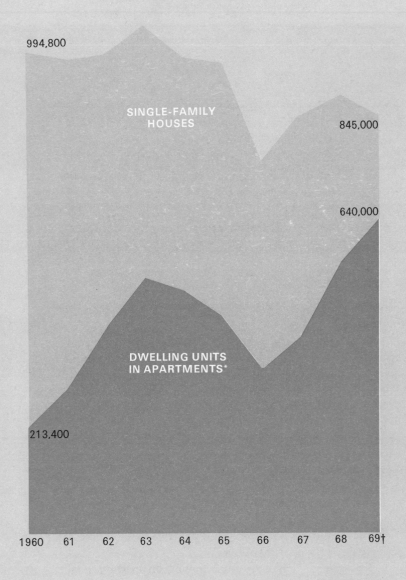

994,800

SINGLE-FAMILY
HOUSES

845,000

640,000

DWELLING UNITS
IN APARTMENTS*

213,400

1960   61   62   63   64   65   66   67   68   69†

†Annual rate, first 10 months.

*Structures with three or more dwelling units.

Source: U.S. Dept. of Commerce, Census Bureau

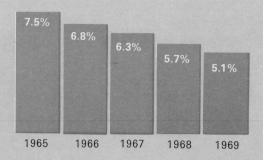

SHRINKING SUPPLY OF RENTALS

**Percentage of Vacancies in Houses
and Apartments Available for Rent**

7.5% | 6.8% | 6.3% | 5.7% | 5.1%

1965　1966　1967　1968　1969

Source: Bureau of the Census, Bureau of Labor Statistics

want to buy, and their employers don't want them to buy either."

—An increase in the age groups that are normally renters—young single people who often double up, young married couples, and elderly people who are anxious to shuck the care and maintenance of a house. Population experts say the number of persons in these age groups is likely to continue to rise significantly during the 1970s. By 1973, for instance, there will be 2.4 million marriages a year—exceeding the stampede to the altar that followed World War II.

Signs like these point toward a continuing boom in apartments—and attract the interest of investors, large and small, all across the country.

For the average investor, there are two basic ways to participate in the apartment boom:

1. You can go it alone, either buying an existing small apartment building; or purchasing a large residence and converting it into apartments.

2. You can join a group, such as a syndicate or real

estate investment trust, and, by pooling funds, undertake construction of large apartment projects.

How to deal in renovated property

Many investors are attracted to the possibility of buying older homes, renovating them into apartments, and then either selling them at a profit or putting them on the market as rental property.

The reasons for the attraction are several. Since the investor probably owns his own home, he feels he already knows something about residential property. Financing is often easier to obtain on residential property than on other kinds of real estate. And since the outlay of cash is smaller than with many other real estate purchases, the risk of financial loss is less.

Some words of caution are in order, however. Authorities say it is almost essential that the investor who deals in renovated residential property know a great deal about construction and repair work. This way he can do some of the work himself and supervise subcontractors without having to hire a general contractor. Also, this type of investment can be time-consuming, and before you embark on this venture you should make certain you have the time available. This type of investment activity has been described as ideal for a retiree who is mechanically inclined. He has the time and talent to make a go of it.

Often, some of the best investment possibilities are to be found in areas not far from the central business section of a city. One of the best known examples is the Georgetown section of Washington, D.C. This area had become rather rundown. But the buildings were structurally sound, and they were architecturally handsome. With the federal payroll expanding, young government executives searching for close-in housing began rehabilitating Georgetown residences, converting some into apartments. Before long, it became the home of many congressmen and top government officials, including the late President John F. Kennedy. Prices in Georgetown have soared in recent years. It is not uncommon for residences there to sell for more than $100,000. The same buildings were selling for one-third that price a few years earlier.

What has happened in Georgetown can—and is—taking place in many other cities across the country. There is, for example, Society Hill in Philadelphia. And there is Old Town in Chicago; a half dozen areas in Brooklyn, N.Y.; Mt. Adams in Cincinnati; several sections of Boston; and the Capitol Hill section of Washington.

Many of these neighborhoods have similar backgrounds. Generally speaking, they once were desirable residential areas built in the last century not far from the downtown section of the city. Then, following World War II, the great exodus to the suburbs began. The once-charming neighborhoods in the central city deteriorated. But now, increasingly large numbers of young families are moving back into renovated residences and apartments in the city. This has caused a rise in the neighborhoods' property values.

Take the Boerum Hill section of Brooklyn. Located about a fifteen minute subway ride from Wall Street, Boerum Hill was built just after the Civil War. For many years, it was a fashionable neighborhood. But gradually it fell into disrepair. Then, about five years ago, young families began moving back to Boerum Hill and renovating the stately residences. In 1966, one house in the neighborhood sold for $16,000. Four years later, it was on the market again. This time the price was $70,000. The same has been true for many other houses in the neighborhood.

By staying alert for the latest housing trends in his city, an investor interested in buying older residences and converting them into apartments may be able to find profitable deals.

Let us take a hypothetical case to illustrate how it can be done:

Claude White, an insurance adjustor, inherited $10,000 from an uncle. He toyed with the idea of investing it in the stock market, but he noticed the market was in one of its periodic downslides. So he began looking around at other investment possibilities. He wanted an investment which would supplement his regular income, and at the same time show capital growth. One day, not far from his office, he noticed a "For Sale" sign on a large, but rather rundown, residence in a nice neighborhood a few blocks from downtown. He noticed that a similar house across the street had been converted into a small but attractive apartment building. He jotted down the telephone number on the "For Sale" sign, and that afternoon he called the real estate broker who was advertising the old house.

The broker explained that the property had been owned by an elderly widow who had died six months earlier. Her heirs wanted to sell the property to settle the estate. The broker did not use the phrase "distress sale," but he made it clear they wanted to sell quickly. "They are asking $30,000," the broker told Mr. White. His tone indicated they might settle for less.

Mr. White made an appointment that weekend to inspect the property. He brought along his brother-in-law, Albert Douglas, an architect who had some experience in renovating older residences. They went over the old house from top to bottom, looking for structural weaknesses and paying special attention to the condition of the foundations, plumbing, heating, and electrical system. Then, later, over a cup of coffee, they compared notes. The house was structurally sound, they decided. It had extensive rewiring not too many years earlier, so its electrical system was in good condition. Plumbing was another matter. It appeared that some repairs might be needed. The old oil furnace in the basement had seen better days.

Mr. White asked his brother-in-law whether the old house could be converted into four apartments. The architect thought it could, and undertook to show how it might be done.

On the back of a paper napkin, he sketched a rough outline of the two-story, 12-room house. Then he indicated how it could be converted into four apartments— one with four rooms, one with three rooms and two with two rooms—without making any major structural changes in the house. Some new doors would have to be cut and other doorways sealed, kitchens and bathrooms installed, and an outside rear staircase added. The inside staircase could be utilized, as well as the kitchen and the two bathrooms.

He estimated that all the renovation, including painting the house inside and out, could be done for $5,000 if costs were watched closely.

Mr. White presented his case to several subcontractors, getting their estimates of the cost of renovating the house. One figured $7,500; another, $6,000; a third, $5,750; and a fourth, $4,950.

Meanwhile, Mr. White was dickering with the real estate broker. He made an offer of $22,500 for the house. The broker, who was asking $30,000, said that was much too low. He agreed to come down to $28,000. Mr. White made a counter-offer of $25,000. The broker said he would have to consult with the administrator of the estate. "Sold," he told Mr. White the next day.

The next step: arranging financing. Mr. White figured he could pay $5,000 down, so he needed to arrange a $20,000 mortgage. Within a few days, he found a lender who was agreeable to making a $20,000, 25-year loan at 7½ percent interest. Monthly payments on the mortgage would be just under $150 a month. Mr. White figured that taxes, insurance, maintenance and other expenses of the property would add perhaps $100 a month to this figure, bringing the monthly outlay to about $250 a month.

What could he rent the apartments for?

After talking with real estate men and apartment managers, and personally inspecting some comparable unfurnished apartments then on the market, he came to these conclusions:

The two-room units could easily be rented at $85 a month; the three-room unit for $100 and the four-room unit for $115. In each case, the tenants would pay their own utility bills. That meant, with all apartments occupied, the building would have gross revenue of $385 a month—or $135 more than the anticipated mortgage payment and expenses.

Mr. White therefore went through with the project. With the help of his brother-in-law, who drew up plans for the renovation and helped supervise the subcontractors, he converted the old house into a four-unit apartment building. Total cost of the renovation was $5,000. Including his $5,000 down payment, the apartment building represented a cash outlay of $10,000.

Three days after the renovation was completed, thanks

to a brightly written ad in the classified section of Sunday's newspaper, he signed four tenants to one-year leases. All the new tenants were interested in renting apartments near the downtown section where they worked, and Mr. White's apartments suited their needs.

This is how Mr. White figured his balance sheet would look after the first year of apartment ownership:

Balance Sheet

Cost of building:	$25,000 ($5,000 cash; $20,000 mortgage)	
Cost of renovation:	5,000 (cash)	
Total cost	$30,000 ($10,000 cash)	
Annual rent on apartments:		
$385 a month × 12 months		$4,620
Annual expenses:		
Mortgage payments	$1,800	
Insurance, taxes, maintenance, etc.	$1,200	
Total expenses		$3,000
	Annual return	$1,620

With all the apartments rented and after paying anticipated expenses, Mr. White would enjoy an annual return of more than 16 percent of his $10,000 cash investment. At the same time, he would be building up a cash equity that he could later sell if he desired.

In this example, Mr. White obeyed several rules which experts say one should follow if he is interested in such an investment. They include:

• Make sure of your location. Mr. White picked a building in a good neighborhood near office buildings and stores where people work and shop. Proximity to work is important to many people.

• Don't "over-renovate." Mr. White kept his renovation plans simple, and his renovation costs low. It usually does not pay to sink too much money into converting a residence into apartment units.

• Make certain the building is structurally sound. In this case, Mr. White and his brother-in-law made a close inspection to insure there were no structural flaws.

• Be sure your rents are comparable. Mr. White decided upon the rents he would charge after making a careful study. He sought as high rental as possible, without charging so much as to price himself out of the market.

• Avoid multi-mortgages. With such an investment, you generally cannot afford the high interest rates charged on second mortgages. Unless you have a large enough cash down payment to avoid placing multi-mortgages on the property, you probably should seek some other kind of investment.

• Be alert to "distress sales." In Mr. White's case, the property needed to be sold to settle an estate, and the heirs were more interested in a quick sale than in holding out for a high price. But remember that an advertisement headed "Owner Must Sell—Sacrifice" sometimes is merely a tactic to get you interested and make you think you are getting a good deal.

Buying existing apartments

Most of these same rules apply if you are interested in purchasing an existing apartment building. Here is another case history to illustrate how it can be done:

Dr. Richard Barnes, a dentist in a medium-sized midwestern city, wanted to put his savings into the kind of investment which would give him tax sheltered income and at the same time allow him to build up an equity which could be sold later when he retired.

He talked to one of his friends, a local real estate broker, who told him about a ten-unit apartment building in the city which was for sale. The broker outlined the deal this way:

The price of the apartment building was $130,000, with $30,000 cash required as down payment. The $100,000 balance could be financed with a twenty-five year, 7 percent interest mortgage. The average rent charged for each of the ten units was $150 monthly, so the building's annual gross income would be $18,000, assuming a 100 percent occupancy. From this he would have to make his mortgage payments ($8,485 a year), plus operating expenses (about $4,500) and taxes (about $1,500). Thus, expenses would total $14,485 a year, leaving a net income of $3,515 a year. That is a return of better than 17 percent on his $30,000 cash down payment.

To show how important it is to calculate expected gross income and anticipated expenses carefully, let us use this same case, but assume that our dentist, Dr. Barnes, failed to do his homework properly.

Suppose occupancy for the year was only 75 percent, instead of 100 percent. That would reduce his gross income to $13,500. Let us assume further that operating expenses ran $1,000 more than expected, or $5,500 instead of $4,500, and that he encountered a $500 tax assessment for street improvements, boosting taxes to $2,000. This would bring his annual expenses to $15,985, including mortgage payments. Thus, Dr. Barnes would pay dearly for his inaccurate calculations. He would lose $2,485 a year instead of making a profit of $3,515.

It is important, too, to pick tenants carefully. Many owners of small apartment buildings check out the prospective tenant's employment and references. Often, they obtain a credit check from a reputable credit investigating firm. And landlords have learned that it is best to require the tenant to make a security deposit to be applied to the cost of repairing or replacing equipment damaged or removed during the tenant's stay.

The lease should spell out specifically the responsibilities of both tenant and landlord. Standard lease forms are readily available, or you may want your lawyer or real estate broker to draw up one for you. In addition to the lease, many landlords print up a list of apartment rules and regulations, and require that the tenant read and sign the list when he signs the lease.

Experts have this advice for prospective landlords: Be specific. Leave nothing to chance. Put everything in writing.

The cases we have cited of success with small apartment buildings are becoming rare these days. The reason? Smaller apartment operations are finding it difficult to compete with larger projects.

The trend: larger projects

The trend has been away from small projects to larger, more efficient operations. Apartment experts say the industry has made the same change as the motel industry—away from the small "Mom and Pop" establishments of the early 1950s to the large motor hotels of today. This trend is expected to continue, with planners predicting that apartment developments will generally take two forms:

—High rise units, usually in or near shopping areas in cities or suburbs. In these will live mainly young single persons or couples, and the elderly.

—Cluster apartments, low-rise garden apartments, and condominiums with much green space and many recreational areas. These will have three and four bedroom apartments for larger families.

Planners say that future apartment developments will be larger, with more extras, and will require better planning. Already, developers are providing plenty of extras to keep tenants happy. Air conditioning has become standard. Carpeting, tennis courts, swimming pools, fancy landscaping, sauna baths and health clubs are getting to be commonplace. Some builders figure they spend between $750 to $1,000 per unit on recreational facilities.

These big projects require big money—so much, in fact, that experts predict that most large multi-family housing projects in the decade of the 1970s will be the domain of group investors. Individual owners, for the most part, will be unable to participate in the market on a competitive basis.

This means that the lone investor who wants to cash in on the trend toward larger projects probably will have to join in a group endeavor, such as:

• Syndicates. These can be small, involving a half dozen or so investors, or large, involving as many as 100 investors. By pooling their funds, these investors are able to participate in the bigger apartment developments.

• Real estate corporations. In these, the investor buys stock in the corporation, which builds and often operates the larger apartment project. Some real estate corporations specialize in apartment buildings; others are more diversified, investing in other projects like office buildings or shopping centers.

• Real estate investment trusts. You also can buy shares in REITs, which have become more popular because they offer certain tax advantages over real estate corporations.

Before you put your money into any of these group endeavors, you should carefully investigate several factors. First, you need to make certain you can have confidence in the promoters or officers of the syndicate, corporation, or REIT. Are they knowledgeable and experienced in real estate development? Do they have a good reputation for professional management? Have they invested any of their own money in the deal?

Second, you should make some personal checks of the real estate investments the group plans to make or already has made. For instance, do the plans seem to fit long-term housing trends in the area? Is there a demand for the type of project to be undertaken? Is the project in a good location? Are the rents in line with comparable rental units?

Above all, you should remember that there are some danger signs to watch out for. Experts list these major ones:

• A high vacancy rate in new buildings. If a garden apartment has not reached 80 percent occupancy within three months after opening, or 90 percent occupancy after six months, this indicates there is an insufficient demand. With a high-rise building, those figures should be reached within six and nine months.

• Rent concessions and reductions. If you find apartment projects cutting their rent, or offering a month's free rent, this may indicate a softening market.

• Overbuilding. Even in growing cities, if too many new units are built in too short a time, some units will remain empty for a period of time. This can ruin an otherwise prudent investment.

The trend toward larger apartment projects has added a new dimension to financing—the participating or partnership loan which gives the lender a share of the revenue, as well as interest on the loan and a return of the principal.

In 1969, for instance, one industry official estimated that 95 percent of the apartment project loans were of the participating variety.

This participating interest is commonly called a "kicker." And the kicker is being used in more than just apartment financing. Among other common kickers are a share of the rent from a shopping center and a portion of the profit from an office building. Large insurance companies, savings banks, and pension funds were among the lenders that began seeking kickers as inflation eroded the value

*These massive towers, with rounded balconies to provide occupants
with a good view of the Chicago River and Lake Michigan, illustrate
the trend in Chicago toward more and more massive buildings, requiring massive sums of investment capital.*

of the dollar and diminished the appeal of fixed returns on investments.

One widely used type of kicker allows the lender to collect a portion of the property's gross income, usually 2 to 3 percent. Obviously, such an arrangement can be rough on a borrower if his project is not fully successful. For this reason, some lenders specify that a certain level of performance be reached before a property has to pay a share of its income as a kicker.

One large insurance company uses this approach: On a typical apartment project loan, it might ask for a 9½ percent interest rate, plus 20 percent of the rental income above 90 percent of the project's "scheduled" level. The "scheduled" level is the income with full occupancy at original rents. This way, insurance company officials say, the apartment developer is not penalized if his project is less than successful. At the same time, however, this type of kicker can give a lender a rich return if inflation or a housing shortage drives rents higher than their scheduled level.

Other lenders were seeking, in addition to their regular interest charges, the rights to buy stock at reduced prices in the company borrowing the money. Still other major lenders were arranging a whole package of kickers—including a percentage of rents above a certain level and a share of ownership in the project being financed.

Just as the big lenders are interested in sharing the ownership of apartment projects, so are many individual families.

Cooperatives and condominiums

Thousands of families, resigned to apartment living but still hankering for something they can call their own, are buying apartment units on a cooperative or condominium basis. These forms of group ownership, combining at least some of the homeowner's financial benefits and the apartment dweller's freedom from maintenance worries, are attracting a growing number of families.

There is a good deal of confusion surrounding the terms "cooperative" and "condominium." There are differences between the two, and a family would do well to investigate carefully to find out which best suits its individual requirements.

Generally speaking, most cooperatives and condominiums are managed similarly. Each member owner has a voice and vote in the group operation. A board of directors is elected by the owners and is in charge of building management. Each owner is responsible for maintaining his own dwelling unit.

In government-aided middle income cooperatives, each owner has one vote regardless of the size of his investment or the number of rooms in his apartment. The private co-op resident and condominium owner, however, has a vote proportionate to apartment investment and size.

Because one mortgage covers the entire cooperatively owned building and owners are not allowed individual mortgages, a co-op buyer makes a cash down payment on a unit and becomes a shareholder in the corporation or trust owning the property. He receives a lease on a specific dwelling unit and, instead of paying rent, he pays monthly maintenance or carrying charges. Mortgage costs, real estate taxes, cost of maintenance, repairs, replacements and administration of cooperatives are budgeted annually and divided among the tenants on a monthly basis according to their investments.

Private co-ops may be profit or non-profit operations. They may be built expressly for co-operative ownership or they may be created by rental tenants who, as a group, buy an apartment building. In New York City, for instance, removal of rental controls from higher priced apartments has resulted in an increasing number of apartment houses being converted to cooperatives.

Although tenants are apt to pay slightly more in maintenance charges than they previously paid in rent, they benefit through tax deductions, a more stable occupancy, and control over maintenance standards. There also is protection against cost increases rising out of such factors as a small supply of available housing. Here is a hypothetical case history showing how a co-op tenant gains tax advantages:

Edward Hill, a business executive whose income is about $25,000 a year, lives in a co-op apartment in a major city. He pays $200 a month for the carrying charges on his apartment. About half of this, or $100, is his share of the taxes and mortgage interest paid by the cooperative corporation which owns the building.

When he files his federal and state income tax returns, he can deduct this portion of his carrying charges. Assuming he is in the 50 percent tax bracket, this means he saves about $50 a month in taxes. In this way, his monthly rent is, in effect, reduced to about $150 a month.

Some cooperatives afford greater tax deductions than others. If the corporation owns just the building—and not the land—the buyer might pay less in a down payment but his maintenance charges may be higher to cover use of the land. And interest charges might be lower because only the building is mortgaged. Where both the land and building are owned by the corporation, a down payment may be larger, maintenance costs may be lower, and the tenant could have higher tax deductions for interest and amortization on the joint property.

When it comes to selling, the resident of a government-aided cooperative usually is required to sell his apartment back to the corporation at book value, while the private co-op owner can sell at the market price, which could include a profit. However, the prospective private co-op buyer may have to meet the approval of the corporation's board of directors.

While the co-op resident functions both as tenant and owner, the condominium dweller is more like a home owner. He takes actual title of his residence in a multi-unit building or complex. His unit carries a separate mortgage, and is taxed just as if it were a single family home. Besides making his own mortgage and tax payments, the condominium owner also pays his proportionate share of operating expenses for common areas, such as hallways, lobbies, and elevators. Whereas the cooperative owner deducts on income tax his proportionate share of interest and taxes paid by the corporation, the condominium owner deducts his personal mortgage interest and tax payments.

The condominium form of ownership has an advantage over the cooperative form. In a cooperative, if one tenant-owner fails to meet his payments, the others generally must take over the defaulted payments. In a condominium, an owner is responsible only for his own mortgage, not for those of other owners.

If the condominium owner wants to sell his unit, he usually is required only to give the other owners a chance to buy at a price offered by a third party.

Tax advantage is one reason for the growing popularity of cooperatives and condominiums. There are tax benefits in most other types of real estate investment. These are examined in the next chapter.

Taxes on
Your Home and Investments

Federal income tax advantages provide a powerful incentive to investing in real estate. This is true whether the property is for personal use, rental to others, or simply to hold in the hope its value will increase.

Some of the tax breaks lower the amount of tax you must pay the government. Others defer, sometimes for many years, a portion of the taxes you must pay. Although you may eventually have to pay these amounts, you will have had use of your money during the deferral period for other profit-making activities.

Your first experience with the tax advantages of real estate ownership usually comes with the purchase of your personal home.

During the time you live in the home you may deduct from your personal income all of the interest you pay on your mortgage and all of the property taxes you pay to your local government. In these days of soaring property taxes and sharply rising interest rates, these deductions are assuming increasing importance to your bank account.

Let us assume you bought a $30,000 house with $6,000 cash and a $24,000 mortgage at 8 percent interest. During an early year of that mortgage, you would pay an average of $150 a month just in interest—or $1,800 for the full

year. Your property taxes for that house could easily
be $600 a year. Filing your tax return, after taking all
other exemptions and deductions, let us say that you and
your spouse are left with $15,000 in taxable income. That
puts you in the 25 percent tax bracket. Deducting $2,400
in mortgage interest and property taxes, you reduce your
tax bill by $600. Even if you could have rented a house
from some other owner for the same monthly payments
you are making as owner—and that is not likely—you
would not get those deductions and your tax bill would
be $600 higher.

These tax advantages are simple to secure, requiring
only a copy of your tax bill and a statement from your
mortgage holder to determine the amounts which are deductible. In examining your mortgage statement, remember to deduct only mortgage interest. You cannot deduct
mortgage principal, mortgage insurance such as is paid on
a Federal Housing Administration mortgage, homeowners
insurance or any payments into an escrow account held
by the mortgage lender. In checking your tax bill, remember that you can only deduct regular property taxes,
not special assessments for such things as sidewalks or
sewers that tend to increase the value of your property.

Calculations of tax advantage become more complicated
when you sell your home.

The principal benefit is that even if you make a profit
on the sale, you do not have to pay taxes on it in the
sale year if you buy another home within one year that
cost at least as much as you realized from the sale of the
previous home.

This tax break means that, as your income continues
to increase, you can continue to purchase better houses
without having to sacrifice any profits you make to taxes.
These taxes, however, are only postponed—not forgotten.
They must be paid if you eventually sell your residence and
do not buy a new one.

Let us follow Lee and Marjorie Starr through a set
of house transactions to see how these tax rules operate:

In 1965, the Starrs bought their first house, a small two-
bedroom bungalow for $15,000. The next year they added
another bedroom for $2,000.

In 1967, the Starrs decided to move to a newer neighborhood. They were able to sell their bungalow for $20,000, and they purchased a four-bedroom ranch house for $25,-000.

At first, it might seem that the Starrs gained $5,000 on the sale of the bungalow—the difference between the $15,-000 they paid and the $20,000 they received. But other factors must be considered before the profit is calculated.

The money they spent adding the third bedroom can be added to the amount they spent on the house—what the Internal Revenue Service calls the "basis" of the house. That made the basis $17,000.

To sell the house, the Starrs had to pay a real estate agent a $1,200 commission. So they actually got $18,800 from the sale. Thus, their actual gain was $1,800.

Since the Starrs purchased their new home within a year of the time they sold the bungalow and since it cost at least as much as they realized from the bungalow sale, they did not have to pay tax immediately on their $1,800 gain from the bungalow sale.

They must, however, subtract that $1,800 gain from the basis price of their new house. The basis therefore comes to $23,200 instead of $25,000. This reduction of basis thus has the effect of postponing the tax on their original gain.

In 1969, the Starrs sold the four-bedroom house for $30,000. The real estate broker earned an $1,800 commission so the Starrs actually realized $28,200 from the sale. Since the basis of the house was $23,200, their gain was $5,000. We can see that $1,800 of this gain is actually carried over from the sale of their bungalow.

Since the Starrs are moving to a smaller community, they were able to buy a new house for only $26,000. Since the new house cost $2,200 less than the house they sold, that meant they had to pay taxes on $2,200 of their gain from the previous sale. But taxes on the other $2,800 of gain were deferred. That deferred $2,800 was subtracted from the basis of the new house in the smaller community, making its basis $23,200.

If the Starrs had spent $500 fixing up the four-bedroom house strictly to make it more salable, they could have deducted that $500 from the amount of gain on which they had to pay taxes in the year of the sale. Thus, they would have paid taxes on $1,700 of gain and deferred $3,300 instead of $2,800.

Fix-up expenses cannot be used to decrease the amount of your over-all gain on a residence sale, but they can be used to reduce the amount of gain on which you must immediately pay taxes. To qualify for this tax benefit, however, your painting or wall-papering or other fixing up must be done during the ninety days ending on the day the contract to sell is signed and must be paid within thirty days after the sale. And they must be strictly fixing up expenses, not improvements such as addition of storm windows.

Even when you must pay taxes on all or part of the gain from sale of your residence, the tax is assessed at the favorable capital gains rate. The capital gains rate is only half the tax rate for ordinary income and, during 1970, is never more than 29½ percent. By 1972, that ceiling will rise to 35 percent because of changes in the tax law made by Congress during 1969. For a person in the 25 percent tax bracket who has a taxable gain of $10,000 from the sale of his residence, the capital gains break means he must pay only $1,250 in tax on the gain instead of the $2,500 he would pay under the ordinary tax rate.

Federal tax law gives you an additional break if you build a new house when you move up the residence ladder. You have eighteen months after the sale of your old house to move into the new residence, rather than the one year granted in the case of a used house. This allows time to construct the new house in case you do not make up your mind where you want to live until the year is almost up. Persons in the armed forces during the year after sale of their old house also can get additional time to find a new residence, depending on specifics of their military service.

The provisions that allow you to defer tax on gains from sale of your residence do not require you to invest the dollars you get from a house sale into the purchase of your new house. In other words, if you own a $20,000 house outright, sell it for cash and buy a $30,000 house, you can get as big a mortgage as is available on the $30,000 and put the bulk of the proceeds from your old house into stocks, your business, or whatever you like. You will still be able to defer the tax on your gains from the sale of the old house.

A person sixty-five years or older may be able to avoid ever paying part or all of the tax on the gain from sale of his residence. To do so, he must have owned and used his house as a principal residence for at least five of the eight years preceding the sale.

If the sale price less expenses of the sale is $20,000 or less, the entire gain can be permanently removed from tax liability. If the amount realized from the sale is more than ·$20,000, part of the gain can be permanently tax-free on a proportional formula. The part that is not tax-free can be at least deferred if another residence is purchased. The taxpayer can elect to remove residence sale gains from tax liability only once in his lifetime. Thus, a person over sixty-five cannot keep buying and selling houses and never pay any tax on his gains. For a married couple using these over-sixty-five tax breaks, only one spouse has to be over sixty-five.

A tax provision that is particularly important in times when mortgage money is tight gives a property seller some relief from the so-called points he may have to pay in order for the buyer of his property to get a mortgage. Tight money causes lenders to charge discounts known as points. Each point is a one-time charge of 1 percent of the amount loaned. The seller must pay any points above one if the buyer is obtaining a mortgage guaranteed by the Veterans Administration or insured by the Federal Housing Administration because the federal government will not let the buyer pay the points.

The amount of points charged by lenders usually rises in times of tight money when federal or state regulations prohibit them from raising interest rates on mortgages to levels they could earn from other investments. In tight money times, if you sold a house on which the buyer was securing a $30,000 mortgage, you might have to pay eight points, or $2,400, to the lender. But you can deduct those points as a selling expense, just as you deduct the real estate broker's commission, in figuring your gain on the sale.

When you must pay points to get a conventional mort-

REAL ESTATE TAXES IN 122 CITIES

How They Compare

City	Tax rate per $1,000 of full market value	Typical tax on $20,000 home	City	Tax rate per $1,000 of full market value	Typical tax on $20,000 home
Alabama			**Illinois** continued		
Birmingham	$ 9.20	$184	Peoria	$20.50	$410
Mobile	7.60	152	Rockford	18.70	374
Montgomery	5.40	108	**Indiana**		
Arizona			Evansville	16.70	334
Phoenix	24.80	496	Fort Wayne	25.60	512
Tucson	23.60	472	Gary	20.70	414
Arkansas			Hammond	21.60	432
Little Rock	11.80	236	Indianapolis	32.10	642
California			South Bend	28.30	566
Anaheim	18.60	372	**Iowa**		
Berkeley	17.40	348	Des Moines	30.60	612
Fresno	21.20	424	**Kansas**		
Glendale	16.60	332	Kansas City	21.70	434
Long Beach	16.00	320	Topeka	24.40	488
Los Angeles	18.50	370	Wichita	25.80	516
Oakland	17.20	344	**Kentucky**		
Pasadena	21.00	420	Louisville	13.90	278
Sacramento	22.70	454	**Louisiana**		
San Diego	20.90	418	Baton Rouge	10.00	200
San Francisco	9.30	186	New Orleans	9.50	190
San Jose	22.20	444	Shreveport		
Santa Ana	18.00	360	(Caddo		
Torrance	18.10	362	Parish)	9.30	186
Colorado			**Maryland**		
Denver	20.30	406	Baltimore	34.70	694
Connecticut			**Massachusetts**		
Bridgeport	14.60	292	Boston	30.60	612
Hartford	27.90	558	New Bedford	25.40	508
New Haven	23.00	460	Springfield	36.80	736
Waterbury	25.90	518	Worcester	38.60	772
D.C.			**Michigan**		
Washington	11.90	238	Dearborn	12.50	250
Florida			Detroit	19.40	388
Jacksonville	33.80	676	Flint	16.80	336
Miami	30.70	614	Lansing	23.60	472
St. Petersburg	31.90	638	**Minnesota**		
Tampa	35.60	712	Duluth	22.70	454
Georgia			Minneapolis	21.20	424
Atlanta			St. Paul	19.80	396
(DeKalb			**Mississippi**		
County)	24.10	482	Jackson	23.70	474
Atlanta			**Missouri**		
(Fulton			Kansas City		
County)	14.70	294	(Clay County)	17.70	354
Columbus	12.60	252	Kansas City		
Savannah	22.90	458	(Jackson		
Hawaii			County)	16.00	320
Honolulu	12.10	242	St. Louis	17.00	340
Illinois			**Nebraska**		
Chicago	19.40	388	Lincoln	29.40	588

City	Tax rate per $1,000 of full market value	Typical tax on $20,000 home	City	Tax rate per $1,000 of full market value	Typical tax on $20,000 home
Nebraska continued			**Pennsylvania** continued		
Omaha	$28.90	$578	Pittsburgh	$16,80	$336
New Jersey			**Rhode Island**		
Camden	32.30	646	Providence	26.50	530
Jersey City	28.50	570	**Tennessee**		
Newark	40.60	812	Chattanooga	19.20	384
Paterson	31.90	638	Knoxville	21.00	420
Trenton	43.10	862	Memphis	20.00	400
New Mexico			Metropolitan Nashville-Davidson	13.30	266
Albuquerque	14.20	284	**Texas**		
New York			Amarillo (Potter County)	19.20	384
Buffalo	30.90	618	Amarillo (Randall County)	18.40	368
New York	20.30	406	Austin	18.40	368
Niagara Falls	31.10	622	Corpus Christi	21.70	434
Rochester	23.90	478	Dallas	14.80	296
Syracuse	29.10	582	El Paso	18.30	366
Utica	37.90	758	Fort Worth	23.20	464
Yonkers	25.30	506	Houston	17.90	358
North Carolina			Lubbock	20.20	404
Charlotte	14.90	298	Wichita Falls (Wichita County)	21.40	428
Greensboro	8.00	160	**Utah**		
Winston-Salem	13.40	268	Salt Lake City	15.80	316
Ohio			**Virginia**		
Akron	17.30	346	Newport News	10.20	204
Canton	14.20	284	Norfolk	11.80	236
Cincinnati	18.60	372	Richmond	15.10	302
Cleveland	17.50	350	**Washington**		
Columbus	14.40	288	Seattle	10.50	210
Dayton	17.80	356	Spokane	15.50	330
Toledo	15.40	308	Tacoma	13.50	270
Youngstown (Mahoning County)	16.00	320	**Wisconsin**		
Oklahoma			Madison	25.70	514
Oklahoma City (Oklahoma County)	18.60	372	Milwaukee	33.10	662
Tulsa (Tulsa County)	20.20	404	122 cities, median tax*	19.80	396
Oregon					
Portland (Multnomah County)	23.70	474			
Pennsylvania					
Allentown	17.30	346			
Erie	13.60	272			
Philadelphia	26 10	522			

Note: Figures are based on a new study conducted by the Census Bureau of property taxes in 122 cities in 1966. Taxes shown here do not take into account partial exemptions in some states on some classes of property.

*Median is the middle figure; tax is higher than the median in half the cities and lower in half.

gage, you may be able to deduct them as interest in your itemized deductions if they are a means of increasing the interest and not simply a fee for specific services given by the lender, such as an appraisal.

If you use your home partly for some purpose other than residence—for example, as a doctor's office—you will only be able to take advantage of these residential tax breaks in proportion to the extent that the property is used as a residence. The rest of the property would be considered in connection within the business section of your tax return.

There is one very important "non-break" to keep in mind about the sale of your own residence: If you lose money on the transaction, you cannot deduct the loss anywhere on your tax return.

Renting your house

Your first experience in operating rental property may well come with your own house. For many reasons— lengthy travel, a bad time for selling, no immediate need for the equity—you may decide to rent out your house when you move, rather than sell it. Even though it is the same house you previously treated as a residence for tax purposes, the tax treatment changes when you convert to rental property.

Basically, you will have to report as income any amounts you receive from the rental of your property. But any expenses you incur in connection with this income may be deducted. These expense deductions often can be handled in such a way that, although you pocket money each month from the rental property, your tax return will show a loss on the rental operation.

How can you appear to lose money while actually making it?

The main reason is the tax break given for depreciation.

Depreciation is the means of recovering your investment in the house. It rests on the theory that the house will wear out in a given number of years. Theoretically, you would set aside the amount of depreciation each year so that when the house did wear out, you would have the money to build a new one. In practice, however, you are likely simply to use depreciation as an accounting device. But since the amount of depreciation allowed in a year may well exceed your amount of real profit on the rental, you will appear to lose money while your bank account actually grows. For example, you may have a $25,000 house which you rent for $250 a month. Your cash expenses such as mortgage, interest, taxes and expenses are $210 a month. Your profit is $40 a month, or $480 for the year. But if your depreciation for the year is $500, you have a tax loss of $20.

Unfortunately for the real estate investor, Congress has placed new restrictions effective in 1970 on the rates at which depreciation can be taken. New housing still can be depreciated at the most favorable rate, but the rate has been curtailed for used housing. If you were converting your residence to rental property, it would of course be considered used housing.

The depreciation rates considered most favorable are those which permit more depreciation to be taken early in the life of the property. These types of depreciation are called accelerated depreciation. The total depreciation, taken over the life of the property, cannot exceed the original value of the property so, if extra depreciation is taken early, less depreciation must be taken later. But by then, you may have sold the property anyhow.

The simplest form of depreciation is called "straight-line." It is called this because the same amount is taken for depreciation each year. Thus, a $20,000 house with a life of forty years would be depreciated at $500 a year.

The accelerated forms of depreciation most often used are called "declining balance" and "sum of the years digits." Under this arrangement, you could claim a depreciation of $1,000 in the first year on that $20,000 house, with declining amounts of depreciation in each successive year.

Highly accelerated depreciation can be applied only to housing that is new. Used housing acquired after July 24, 1969, must be depreciated at a lower rate—and then only if it has at least 20 years of life remaining. Such housing with a shorter useful life must now be depreciated by the straight-line method.

The lot on which the house sits cannot be depreciated inasmuch as land is a permanent asset. Thus, you may have paid $27,000 for the property—$7,000 for the land and $20,000 for the building. When you convert your residence to rental property, you must determine your basis for depreciation. This usually would be the amount that you paid for the property minus the value of the land, plus your costs of acquiring the property and the value of permanent improvements you made on the house. If this figure is higher than the fair market value of the house at the time you convert it to rental use, then you must use the fair market value as your basis for depreciation. You might have to use fair market value if, for example, the house were in a declining neighborhood or if you added costly improvements whose value you could not recapture when selling the house.

Other than depreciation, deductible expenses in operating rental property are essentially those costs you actually incur. These are usually subdivided into "repairs" and "other expenses." Repairs and maintenance are the things you do that do not add appreciably to the value, utility, or useful life of the property. This would include such items as fixing a leaky sink, replacing a broken window, or repairing a hole in the roof. You cannot deduct as repairs such items as adding a shower to a bathroom or erecting a fence around the house. Since these add to the value of the property, they must be depreciated over a number of years.

Heading the list of your other expenses which are deductible will be taxes and, if you have a mortgage, the interest you pay on it. You can also deduct such expenses as commissions for collecting rent, as well as advertising, utilities, fire and liability insurance, expenses of your travel to inspect or maintain the property, and mortgage insurance such as you pay if you have a mortgage guaranteed by the FHA.

You will have to prorate your depreciation and certain of your expenses if you turn your residence into rental property at any time other than the start of your tax year. If you convert halfway through the tax year, you can deduct depreciation, insurance, and similar expenses only for the second half of the year. If you repaired something in the second half of the year, you can deduct all of that expense—but you cannot deduct anything for repairs made before you started to rent out the property. You also must prorate your deductions if you convert only a part of your residence to a rental—for example, if you rent out the upstairs. If you rent out half your house, you could deduct half of the depreciation, repairs, taxes, mortgage interest, utilities, and other expenses attributable to the whole house. Half of mortgage interest and taxes attributable to half of the house in which you live could be deducted as part of your itemized deductions.

Renting other property

You may be so successful in renting your former residence that you may want to expand your rental operations. The tax principles are the same whether you are renting out a two-bedroom house, a garden apartment building, or a high-rise office building: You may deduct your depreciation, repairs, and other expenses, and you must declare all your income from the rental. Again, the tax advantage of depreciation is that it often will cancel out, for tax purposes, all or much of the cash you pocket, meaning those dollars are tax-free, at least for the present.

Depreciation rules vary for different types of buildings, however. Under the Tax Reform Act of 1969, Congress restricted the very favorable 200 percent declining balance rate of accelerated depreciation to new housing, including apartments. Formerly, this rate was available for all new construction. Other new construction now can be depreciated no faster than under the 150 percent declining balance rate. Thus, a $100,000 apartment building with a fifty-year life span could be depreciated $4,000 in the first year using the 200 percent rate, but a $100,000 office building with the same life could be depreciated only $3,000 using the 150 percent rate. Each building, of course, could be depreciated its full value over its full life, but more of the apartment's value could be depreciated in early years.

A used building which you acquire must be depreciated at the straight-line rate unless it is used for housing and has a life span of at least twenty years remaining. Then it can be depreciated at the 125 percent declining balance rate.

You may become involved with numerous other depreciation schedules beyond that for the building itself if you provide furniture, equipment or other personal property. You can depreciate all but the salvage value of these items over the period of their useful life. The Treasury Department offers guidelines on what to consider as a reasonable useful life for items, but will normally accept your declaration of useful life if you can show it is in line with your replacement practices. For example, it suggests a ten-year life for office furniture, but likely would accept your useful life declaration of eight years if you show that you, in fact, replace the furniture that often.

When you move into bigger scale rental operations, the scope of your other deductible expenses may broaden. You may pay a property manager; you may retain a lawyer and an accountant; you may hire maintenance or service employes; you may have court fees or other municipal costs. All these are deductible.

Selling your rental property

If you have held your rental property for longer than six months and then sell it, you get a tax break on the profits you make from the sale: You pay tax on your profit at only half the ordinary tax rate. This is because your profit is considered a long-term capital gain. If you are in the very top income brackets, you may even pay at a rate of less than half for profits taken during 1970 and 1971 as new provisions of the Tax Reform Act of 1969 are phased into operation. Starting in the 1972 tax year, however, the capital gain tax rate will be one-half the rate of each tax bracket, including the highest.

If you sell rental property after holding it six months or less, your gain is taxed at the ordinary income rates. Thus, if you bought a building on January 1, sold it June 30 for a $3,000 gain and you were in the 36 percent tax bracket, you would pay $1,080 in tax. But if you waited until July 2 to sell it, your tax on the same gain would be only $540.

If you have converted your house to rental property, however, you may count as part of the six months the time you used the house for your own residence.

In calculating your gain on the sale of rental property, you determine your basis of the property by totaling your purchase price and subsequent improvements, and subtracting from this the depreciation you have taken on the building. You determine the proceeds you realized from the sale by subtracting your selling costs from the sales price. The excess of the proceeds over the basis is your gain.

If you have used accelerated depreciation on your rental property, a portion of your gain may be taxed at the ordinary income rate rather than the more favorable capital gains rate.

You will recall that using accelerated depreciation enabled you to reduce your taxes during the years you held the building for rental. But, as noted above, depreciation must be subtracted from the original price of the building in calculating your basis. Since total depreciation under an accelerated plan is higher than under the straight line depreciation until you have fully depreciated the building, your basis will be lower if you have used accelerated depreciation. With a lower basis, your gain on the sale is more. When you sell, tax law requires you to calculate the difference between the accelerated depreciation you took and the amount which depreciation would have totaled had you used straight line. This portion of your gain is then taxed at ordinary rates. This means that you are paying back some or all of the tax you saved in previous years by using accelerated depreciation.

The amount of this depreciation difference—called excess depreciation—which is subject to the ordinary tax rate can be reduced if your rental property was housing and you held it for at least eight years and four months. For each month after that, one percent of the excess depreciation is thrown back into the capital gains tax rate. After sixteen years and eight months, all of the excess depreciation is back in capital gains and you have fully benefited from accelerated depreciation without ever having to pay the deferred tax.

If you have used straight-line depreciation, none of your gain is subject to ordinary tax rates.

In previous years, ordinary tax on excess depreciation could be completely eliminated after ten years for all types of buildings. But the Tax Reform Act of 1969 limited this privilege to housing and extended the elimination period to sixteen years and eight months.

If you are selling your rental property and plan to purchase other rental property, you may be able to avoid taxes on the gain by negotiating an exchange. In an ideal exchange of properties of equal value, there would be no tax liability. Your basis on the first property would simply become the starting point for figuring your basis on the new property when you eventually sold it. Exchange of property with some cash or other consideration thrown in can be handled partially tax-free.

You can defer paying tax on your full gain if you make a deferred payment sale of property. Your sale can qualify for this tax treatment if you do not receive more than 30 percent of the sales price in the year of the sale. Then you pay tax only on the proportion of the profit realized in the first year and in each year thereafter as you are paid off. If you receive more than 30 percent of the payment in the first year, you must pay any tax on your full gain in that year.

So far, we have assumed you made a profit on the sale of your rental property. What happens if you lose money?

You may recall that a loss on the sale of your residence is not deductible. However, a loss on investment property *is* deductible because it is considered a capital loss and can be used to offset other capital gains, such as you might have from profits on other property or on stocks and bonds. If you cancel all your capital gains with capital losses, you can deduct half of the remaining capital loss from your ordinary income up to a $1,000 maximum in the year. Excess capital losses may be carried over to future years as offsets to gains on ordinary income.

Holding and selling land

Land transactions may bring capital gains tax breaks such as those on sales of buildings. But you will not get depreciation benefits because land is not depreciable—its useful life is indefinite.

If you purchase land and rent it out—for example, as an unimproved parking lot—you handle your taxes much the same as if you rented a building. You must declare all income, but you deduct all expenses such as mortgage interest, taxes, and maintenance.

If you purchase and hold unimproved and unproductive land, you have a choice of how to handle your expenses. They may be deducted each year, giving you a loss on the land holding, or they may be "capitalized"—added to the cost of the land. Factors such as your other income and your plans for the land would influence this choice. Once you turn the property to productive use, however, the deductible expenses can no longer be capitalized.

When you sell land, your gain is considered a capital gain—if you have held the land for more than six months and if buying and selling land is not your business (as it is with a real estate agent). Losses on land deals are deductible in the same way as capital losses on buildings discussed earlier.

Your trickiest tax problems could come if you subdivide a tract of land and sell the lots. The Treasury Department may consider you as a land dealer and tax your gain at the ordinary income rates unless you can meet certain conditions. Included are requirements that you held the property for at least five years, and made no substantial improvement in the land and you were not holding any other property for sale to customers in the ordinary course of trade or business. Any improvement that increases the value of the property by more than 10 percent may be considered substantial unless you can convince the Treasury otherwise. If you have held property ten years or longer, you can make somewhat more extensive improvements, such as installation of water, sewer, drainage facilities, hard surface roads, curbs and gutters. But erecting a commercial building would be considered a substantial improvement.

If you meet those conditions, then you can sell lots and not have the gains taxed at the ordinary rate. If you sell five or fewer lots, all the profit is capital gains. If, in the same year, you sell more than five lots, a portion of the gain on these additional lots may be taxed at the ordinary rate, depending on your selling expenses.

You may purchase land with oil or other mineral value and lease it to producers for what is called a royalty. These royalties are ordinary income, but your tax can be reduced by depletion allowances. A depletion allowance is a tax break which is designed to compensate you for the fact that the production of the oil or other mineral is depleting your holdings of it. Tax calculations in this area can become extremely complex, but such allowances have successfully been applied by some oil operators to reduce their tax bills substantially.

If you buy timberland, assuming that timber is not your ordinary business, and then you sell the timber after holding the land for longer than six months, you can get favorable capital gains treatment on the profits. Under some situations, you can also get capital gains treatment for selling coal or iron ore on your land.

Farms

The Tax Reform Act of 1969 restricted the practice by which wealthy individuals could operate a farm at a loss, then deduct the loss from their nonfarm ordinary income. Because tax law permits some expenses to be deducted in farming while requiring them to be capitalized in other industries, farm losses that were losses only on paper could be created. Under the new law, individuals with nonfarm income in excess of $50,000 will be taxed under tougher rules. Annual farm operating losses in excess of $25,000 will be cumulated over the years ahead and future gains from the sale of farm land and certain other farm property will be taxed as ordinary income to the extent of the cumulated operating losses. For the taxpayer in a lower income bracket, the lure of any tax breaks would have to be weighed against the risks and investment required in that business.

Record keeping and timing

Precise record keeping and careful attention to timing of your real estate dealings are vital if you are to realize fully the tax benefits which are available. If your tax return is audited, the Treasury will not accept "guesstimates" and unverified figures for deductions you claim. If you do not keep up-to-date records with supporting documents, you may forget to claim some of the deductions you are entitled to.

Even if you own nothing more than your house, keep records. What about that $100 fence you put up in your back yard three years ago? Now that you are selling the house, you could add that cost to your basis and cut your amount of gain on the sale. But if you do not have a receipt and cannot remember what contractor did the work, you will be out of luck trying to substantiate the deduction.

If you are active in real estate investments, you likely will have an accountant or tax lawyer prepare your tax returns for you. But you will have to supply him with complete records so he can get you all the tax allowances to which you may be entitled.

Accurate records will also help you to plan the timing of your transactions. Frequently, your decisions will be affected by other income. If you know that your income will be lower next year than in the current year, you may want to prepay property taxes or other expenses so that you can use the deductions to offset this year's higher tax bracket income. Or if you know your income is going to rise next year, it may be wise to delay paying a bill for improvements until after the first of the year. The pattern of other income may affect your choice between taking straight-line or accelerated depreciation. In short, accurate records are essential for real estate investments.

The Tax Reform Act of 1969 curtailed some of the tax advantages of real estate investment. But enough tax breaks remain to provide a powerful incentive to investment in real estate.

PART TWO

Buying a House

How to Assess
Your Housing Needs

We are a nation of homeowners.

More than 64 percent of all American families own their own homes, and the percentage is growing. In a typical year, 4.5 million families buy a house—or an average of one every ten seconds around the clock. At the same time, millions more are considering such a step.

Perhaps you are one of these millions in the market for a house. Maybe you are concerned with such needs as an extra room for the new baby, or good schools for the older children, or a better kitchen for the wife.

There are many reasons for wanting to buy a house. Usually, a buyer has two types of motives: the practical kind you can list without much trouble, and the hidden psychological motives that you may not even know you have.

Let us consider a typical young family and their motives for wanting to buy a house:

Tom and Judy Howard (the names are fictitious but the circumstances are real) live in a two-bedroom apartment with their two-year-old son Tommy. They have saved $4,000, and figure this is enough for a down payment on a house. They feel it is time to buy a house in a nice suburb so Tommy can have a safe yard to play in. They think they would enjoy owning their own house. And Tom thinks they might save money because they "won't be throwing away all the money in rent." Besides, he was a whiz at woodworking in high school, and he would like to own and use some power tools.

Thus, the Howards' motives range from practical to personal to psychological. They are not unlike the motives of millions of others who are in the market for a house. A survey conducted a few years ago by the United States Savings and Loan League found that the dominant motives for homeownership are non-economic.

Of every 100 reasons given, 38 can be classed as economic. When asked why they wanted to buy their own home, 22 percent of the respondents said buying enables one to build an equity in real estate. Ten percent replied that when you rent you have nothing to show for it but receipts from your landlord. Six percent stated that buying a house is cheaper than renting.

The other reasons given for homeownership in the survey are non-economic and tied to the family's social and personal needs. Among these reasons were the desire to provide a better environment for children, privacy, freedom to improve the property, and the need for more space. Several husbands simply said that their wives wanted to own a home.

Should you buy or rent?

If you are like most families, buying a home is the biggest purchase you will ever make. You would indeed be foolish not to spend ample time trying to get the best answers to basic questions like:

What are your personal and family needs?

How much can you afford to spend?

How can you make sure you are getting the most for your money?

There is one question that should be answered before all others:

Should you buy a house? Or, as it is often phrased, should you buy or rent?

This is a highly personal decision. There is no magic

Left:
The ideal of millions of Americans—a typical middle-class home in suburbia, this one in Springfield, Virginia, in the vicinity of the nation's capital.

Below:
For those who prefer living in the city, a newly developed residential area of Washington, D.C., offers this housing complex.

formula to follow in reaching it. There are disadvantages and advantages to be considered.

Here, as housing experts see them, are the advantages of homeownership:

• A sense of security. For many people, homeownership gives a sense of security. A homeowner is his own master, free from the whims of a landlord. Owning a house also imparts what psychiatrists call "a sense of belonging." Homeowners often say they enjoy the feeling of being a part of the community. They take pride in ownership and find satisfaction in maintaining and preserving their property.

• Better housing and neighborhood. The average homeowner enjoys living conditions superior to those of the average apartment dweller. The homeowner usually has, for example, more living space, more rooms, more household appliances, more storage space, a private garage or parking place, and a backyard for recreation. In addition, a neighborhood of private homes is generally a better place to live than the areas of large apartment buildings. There are fewer people living on each block. This means less congestion, less traffic, and less noise.

• Investment. The money used to buy a house becomes what is widely regarded as one of the soundest investments a family can make. Part of each monthly payment is a form of regular and forced savings which increases the amount of the investment. In periods of inflation, the homeowner is a borrower who repays dollars of declining value. And inflation tends to increase the price of a house.

• A better credit rating. Homeownership generally improves your credit rating. The fact that you own a home is, in itself, often considered a sign of financial stability.

• Tax advantages. The tax deductions available to homeowners are substantial. The interest on the mortgage, plus local and state real estate taxes, are deductible in computing federal income taxes. These deductions can be sizable, especially in the first few years when a big chunk of the monthly mortgage payment is interest. If the house is sold, it is possible to defer the tax due on any profit. And if the house is damaged by fire, flood or like causes, the homeowner can deduct for tax purposes the cost of repairs not covered by insurance.

In capsule form, these are the major advantages of homeownership. But there also are disadvantages which should be weighed before you make the big decision. They include:

• Limitations on relocation. Your flexibility is curtailed when you buy a home. If the family breadwinner is offered a better job in another city, you can move earlier and easier when you rent than when you own. Similarly, if you live in a neighborhood that suddenly starts to go downhill, you can move out if you rent. But if you own your home, you may be forced to stay on, or to sell at what could be a big loss.

• Financial risk. When you rent, the financial risk is limited. You are responsible for rent payments for the life of your lease, no longer. When you buy a house, you are committed to regular mortgage payments for a number of years—no matter what happens to you financially. If you fail to make your payments, you could lose a substantial investment in payments already made.

• Extra work and expense. When you rent, you don't have to worry about the cost of repairs. That comes out of the landlord's pocket. The homeowner also faces tasks like mowing the lawn, raking leaves, shoveling snow, painting the house, repairing the gutters. True, many homeowners enjoy these activities. But other homeowners do not and have to hire help.

• Drain on savings. In addition to the high recurrent expenses of maintaining a home, the initial purchase usually involves a substantial outlay of cash. There is the down payment, plus closing costs, legal fees, and other expenses which will deplete your savings. You may be reluctant to part with your hard-earned savings if you anticipate the need for substantial sums of money in the near future—a child's college education, for example.

Those are the pros and cons of homeownership. Which, then, is best for your family: Buy or rent?

Both sides have valid points. It is the particular circumstances of your family that make one course wiser than the other. So, before making the final decision, it is sensible to consider carefully the arguments on each side.

There is another economic fact-of-life that you should keep in mind—inflation generally benefits the homeowner.

Inflation is defined as a decline in the purchasing power of money. In the United States, the inflationary trend has been almost continuous since the end of the great depression of the 1930s. While inflation erodes the value of the dollar and thus hurts people on fixed incomes, it is highly favorable to those who are in debt. Since the debt is a fixed number of dollars, the debtor finds it easier to get the dollars he needs to repay his debt as dollars become less valuable.

Most homeowners are debtors. They borrow money to buy their homes. As the value of the dollar declines, the homeowner finds it easier to make his mortgage payments. In addition, the value of his home will rise but there will be no corresponding increase in the mortgage debt. As a result, the homeowner may benefit from an inflationary situation.

A dramatic illustration can be found in the case of the first house on which the Federal Housing Administration insured the mortgage. This property was valued by the FHA in 1934 for $7,300. The mortgage was paid off long ago, and now the house is conservatively valued at more than $26,000, although only $2,000 worth of capital improvements, including landscaping, have been added.

Still other statistics paint a picture of steadily rising housing costs. Coupled with the fact that buying a house requires a substantial outlay of cash, this can make the problem of deciding whether to buy or to rent an even more difficult one. Experts say you should not be intimidated by the size of the purchase. A house may appear to be the largest purchase a family makes only because houses are sold in advance. Actually, a family may spend as much money over the years for automobiles as it does for a home. Another comparison might be made: If you signed up in advance for a 25-year supply of food for your family, the figure might be as high or higher than the price of your house.

If, after you buy a house, you conclude you have made a mistake, you need not be too upset. Just as millions of

Americans buy a home every year, so do other millions sell a home. Always, it seems, someone is ready to move into the house that has just been left vacant. This is likely to happen in your case, too.

One reason that you need not worry much about having a vacant, unsold house on your hands is that mobility has become a way of life in the United States. The age of the "ancestral home" is no more. In centuries gone by, the family home was passed from generation to generation. Today, only about 3 percent of the people live their entire lives in the same house. Of the 159 million Americans five years of age or over at the time of the last census, nearly half were living in a house different from the one they had occupied five years earlier. In fact, studies have shown that the typical family stays in the same house only 6 years.

Changing cycles of family life

Experts who have charted the patterns of family life in America report that the housing requirements of a typical family change every five or ten years. Here, in brief, are their findings:

—One to five years after marriage: All living requirements might be satisfied with an efficiency or one-bedroom apartment, or a small house.

—Five to ten years after marriage: The arrival of one or two children requires two or three bedrooms, larger living space, and more storage.

—Ten to fifteen years after marriage: The average family with three children needs still more sleeping space, a second bath, larger living space.

—Fifteen to twenty-five years after marriage: The children are growing up; this ten-year span is generally a more stable period as far as housing requirements are concerned.

—Twenty-five to forty years after marriage: On the average of once every five years, a son or daughter leaves home for college or marriage. Housing needs decline.

—Forty years or more after marriage: The family is down to two persons, who require no more space than in the early years of marriage.

Let us translate these changing cycles of family life into case histories.

Case One: John and Sue Evans are newlyweds. After their honeymoon, they rented a one-bedroom apartment not far from the downtown area where they work—John as an accountant and Sue as a secretary. Their housing needs are simple, so they picked an apartment building with a swimming pool on the roof and with individual balconies. They are near enough to their jobs that both could walk to work in the morning. They figure their apartment will suit their needs until children start arriving a few years from now.

Case Two: Ed and Carol Brown used to live in a downtown apartment, too. But with Carol expecting their first child, they decided to move to a small house in the suburbs. There, the new child can have his own nursery. And Carol wants a family room open to the kitchen so she can keep an eye on the baby when he starts walking. And both Ed and Carol want a yard so that Ed, Jr. can play outside on warm days.

Case Three: Peter and Sylvia Murray have two children, ages six and three, and their two-bedroom house is getting a little crowded. The children—a boy and a girl—need separate bedrooms, and Sylvia has been noticing lately that there is just not enough closet space for the family's multiplying possessions. So, after looking over the market, they decide to buy a bigger, four-bedroom house in a new subdivision. The extra bedroom will come in handy as a combination sewing room for Sylvia and an office for Peter. And it can become a nursery if the family gets a new member.

Case Four: Paul and Janice Smith have been living in their four-bedroom subdivision home for eight years. They have three children—a teen-age boy, an 11-year-old girl, and a 7-year-old boy. Paul has been quite successful as a business consultant, and he has decided they can now afford the "dream house" they always wanted. It should be big enough so they can entertain a number of guests with ease. And it should have widely separated living areas so Paul and Janice can relax undisturbed by their children romping in another part of the house.

Case Five: Henry and Joan Edwards are in their mid-50s. Their children have all graduated from college and have married. They feel that their big house in the suburbs, with its large yard, is simply too much for them to maintain. They decide to move into a new cooperative apartment close to the downtown area. There Mr. Edwards will not have to worry about mowing the lawn every weekend. They will be nearer the theater and the concerts they enjoy. And Mr. Edwards will not have to fight bumper-to-bumper traffic for two hours going to and returning from work.

Case Six: Claude Jones retired recently, and he and his wife, Martha, are heading south to the little house on the beach they purchased some years ago as a vacation home. It is perfect for a retirement home, they decided, since the weather in the area is sunny and warm most of the year. And Mr. Jones will be able to indulge in his favorite sport, fishing.

Each of these cases differs and underscores the fact that family needs change.

Studies of family patterns by housing experts suggest that generally it is best to think of your family's housing requirements in terms of a limited number of years—ten, fifteen, or even twenty years. Keep in mind that your selection of a house should recognize the predictable changes in family life.

Another key factor to be considered is your job outlook.

Are you likely to be transferred to another city? If so, then you probably would buy with only your present family cycle in mind.

Are you settled in for a lifetime career in your present position? If so, then you can safely look ahead at future stages in family cycles.

Is your career still in the making? Are you awaiting other opportunities—across town, in another city or another state? Then you should take special care to buy a house you can sell quickly, without financial sacrifice, when the time comes to move to a new locale.

Fit your house to your style of living

Your style of living is another major consideration when

it comes to determining your family's housing needs. This is why, when you ask an architect to design a home for you, one of the first things he does is to find out as much as he can about each member of the family.

To illustrate how important your living style can be in relation to your housing needs, let us consider three imaginary families. The statistical picture is the same for all three. Each family is composed of five members—husband, wife, and three children aged sixteen, twelve, and seven. Each has an annual income in the $12,000 to $15,000 range. But each has different housing needs.

First, the Harpers.

Ed Harper is with an advertising agency. He often has clients out for dinner, and his wife, Mary, holds several large parties each year. The Harpers entertain a lot, so what they need is a large living area, perhaps opening into a paved terrace through sliding glass doors, as well as to the family room-kitchen on the other side. Then their parties can spread out, with enough room for everyone. The Harpers' children are all girls. They get along reasonably well together, so three bedrooms may be sufficient. But two bathrooms are the minimum. If possible, there should be a half-bath, convenient for guests. The bedrooms and other bathrooms should be as far as possible from the area where the parties are held.

Next, the Yardley family's living style.

Fred Yardley is a salesman who travels a good deal. When he is home on weekends, he likes to take it easy around the house, puttering in the yard and playing with the children—all boys. Since most of his business contacts are out of town, he does not entertain much at home. Sometimes, though, a few friends are invited for dinner. Ann Yardley enjoys cooking, so this family should have a well-equipped kitchen with eating space, plus a separate dining room. The family also wants a family room separated from the living room, so Fred and Ann can relax in the living room away from the boys' horseplay in the family room. And Fred needs a study where he can write up his reports and do other office work. So the Yardleys want at least four bedrooms, with one serving as Fred's study.

Finally, the Daniels family.

Henry Daniels is active in community affairs, is an amateur photographer and a do-it-yourselfer of considerable skill. His wife, Angela, teaches piano at home. All three children are bright students who actually enjoy doing their homework. So the Daniels' needs are obvious. Henry needs space for a darkroom, plus a workshop for his woodworking tools. Angela needs a living room with space for a piano away from the family room. And the children need bedrooms large enough so they can study comfortably by themselves. When the Daniels entertain, it is at informal parties rather than formal dinners so they do not need a separate dining room.

These examples indicate why it is important to pause and think about your family's living style before embarking on serious house-hunting.

How much space do you need?

Too often, families start house-hunting with only a few of their basic needs in mind: The number of bedrooms and bathrooms, the approximate kitchen and dining requirements, and a vague idea of the size lot they want.

And often it is a wife's complaint about a shortage of space that sends a family in search of a new house.

Just what does the wife mean when she says she wants more space? This is one of those vague phrases that bears investigating because so many families move to get more space. Some buyers pick one house over another on the basis of floor space, or "square footage."

How do you know what "square footage" is in a house?

Definitions vary. Some builders count the space in a carport as part of the living space. Others count outside storage space. Still others count the space of a patio. Generally, however, square footage is measured from the outside edge of all walls. Even this can be tricky. In a house 40 feet long and 30 feet wide, about 90 square feet will be taken up in the eight-inch thick outside walls—or 7.5 percent of this 1,200 "square foot" house.

You can easily become a better judge of your space needs by doing a bit of homework. Ask yourself these questions:

How large is the living room of your present home? In your next home, do you want a larger one, or a smaller one? How much larger, or how much smaller?

How many bedrooms do you now have? What is their size? Are they big enough, or are they too small? How much larger, or smaller, should they be?

What about bathrooms? How many do you have now? How many do you think you need?

And the kitchen—is your present one too small? Do you need more counter space, or more drawers? Do you want eating space in the kitchen?

What about a separate dining room? Is it on your list of musts?

How much closet space do you presently have? Is it sufficient? If not, how much more do you need?

Does your family have any special requirements? Have you any hobbies, like photography or ceramics, that need special space and facilities? Are you a do-it-yourselfer, with need for workshop space?

Do you require storage space for bulky equipment like boats, bicycles, or trampolines?

Are there any special needs in your family for invalids or older persons, perhaps in wheel chairs?

These questions deal with the house itself. But what about the land the house sits on? How big should your lot be?

Perhaps you are thinking in terms of an acre. That is 43,560 square feet. It could measure 208 feet by 208 feet, or 100 feet by 435 feet. You may hear the term "acre zoning." This usually means a lot has been rounded off at 40,000 square feet, or 8 percent less than an acre.

But most people settle for less than an acre, or even a rounded-off acre. In some areas, a great majority of houses are built on lots of less than 10,000 square feet. In others, most houses are built on lots of 15,000 to 25,000 square feet.

In southern states, lots often are smaller because the lawn needs to be tended almost year-round. In the north, a lawn needs mowing only four or five months a year, so the lots tend to be a little larger.

One point to keep in mind: It seldom makes sense

to tie up either too little or too much money in the land your house sits on.

Most new houses represent 80 to 85 percent of the total value of the house and land. For example, if your lot has a market value of $3,000, housing experts say the house itself should not cost less than $12,000, for you will not be making full use of the value of the property. And if the cost of the house itself is over $17,000, they say you may be over-building for the neighborhood and not be able to sell for as much as your total $20,000 investment.

Draw up a shopping list

When you go to the supermarket to do your grocery shopping, you probably take along a shopping list.

Unless you have an extraordinary memory, you will find a "shopping list" just as handy when you go shopping for a house. To help you draw up your housing shopping list, run down this checklist. It will help you determine your elementary needs.

1. We will need at least:
    _____ Two bedrooms
    _____ Three bedrooms
    _____ Four bedrooms
    _____ More than four bedrooms
2. We will need:
    _____ One bathroom
    _____ One and one-half bathrooms
    _____ Two bathrooms
    _____ Two and one-half bathrooms
    _____ Three or more bathrooms
3. We will need a garage or carport for:
    _____ One car
    _____ Two cars
    _____ More than two cars
    _____ We don't have a car
4. Because of our special interests, we will need these special rooms:
    _____ Study
    _____ Workshop
    _____ Sewing room
    _____ Game room

_____ Music room

_____ Studio

5. We need extra space to provide for storage of:

_____ Boat or canoe

_____ Books, records

_____ Piano or organ

_____ Power tools

_____ Sports gear

_____ Other

6. For our family's social life, we need facilities for:

_____ Indoor entertaining

_____ Outdoor entertaining

_____ Both

_____ Neither

7. Besides the house, we want:

_____ A large yard with garden space

_____ A small lawn

_____ As little yard space as possible

8. To get to work, we are willing to spend:

_____ Less than half an hour each way

_____ Up to an hour each way

_____ Up to one and one-half hours each way

This checklist covers some of your elementary needs. Other features will come to mind. It is a good idea to jot these down. Then divide these features into two categories: those you feel you cannot do without, and those which are not rock-bottom necessities, but which would make living more pleasant.

You will find that the line dividing your needs and desires often is a thin one. One suggestion: Resolve any differences on your shopping list before—not after—you start house-hunting.

How Much Should You Spend?

How much can you afford to spend for a house?

You should ask yourself that question as you begin to think seriously about buying a house. And it is best to arrive at an answer before you start looking.

Modern mortgage financing has made it possible for most American families to buy a home principally on credit, and a majority do so. You will need some cash for a down payment and other expenses, but no longer does the size of your cash bankroll govern how much of a house you can afford.

This is not meant to imply that cash is of little importance. Cash still remains a consideration. But the old rules have fallen by the wayside over the years. At one time, a person customarily would put up at least half the house's purchase price in cash, taking a mortgage on the other half. Later it became the general rule that one-third cash was required, with a mortgage equal to two-thirds of the value of the house. Nowadays, with government-supported mortgage programs, many families can buy a home with a down payment of 10 percent or less—or, in some cases, with no down payment at all.

The size of the mortgage you can obtain probably will govern how much you will spend for a house. Remember this: experienced mortgage lenders will not let you borrow more than you can afford to repay. The lender is interested in getting his money back, plus interest and fees. He does not want to end up with a foreclosed house on his hands; he is in the lending business, not in the business of selling houses. He does not like to foreclose, and he will do so only under extreme circumstances.

Let us look at the methods the lender uses to decide whether you can pay for the home you want him to finance. Knowing a few facts now can save you the heart-ache of finding that "dream house" only to discover later that you cannot get the loan you need to buy it.

Rules of thumb

There are several, often-repeated rules of thumb on how much you can afford to spend for a house. We will cite them here, but you should bear in mind that no two homeowning families are precisely alike. These rules of thumb should serve as rough guides only, nothing more.

The first of these rules is a simple theory that you cannot afford to pay more than 2½ times your annual income for a home. A second, often-cited rule is that your annual housing costs—including principal and interest payments on the mortgage, real estate taxes, and fire insurance premiums—should not total more than one-fourth of your yearly income.

These two formulas work out about the same. Under them, assuming you must depend entirely on your income to buy a house, this is roughly what you can afford to spend for a house:

Annual Income	Top Price of House
$ 5,000	$12,500
6,000	15,000
7,000	17,500
8,000	20,000
9,000	22,500
10,000	25,000
12,000	30,000
15,000	37,500
20,000	50,000
25,000	62,500

Government studies indicate that, when families get into higher income brackets, they devote a smaller percentage of their income for housing.

One survey found that an average family with a monthly after-tax income of $250 spent $85 a month for housing—mortgage payments, insurance, taxes and utilities. That is 34 percent—well above the oft-cited 25 percent guideline.

The same survey showed that families with $500 monthly income spent an average of $118 for housing, or 24 percent of their income; while families with incomes of $1,000 a month spent an average of $160 a month for housing, or 16 percent.

In addition, there is a wide spread in any income group. Of families earning $750 a month, for example, one-fourth spent less than $126 a month for housing, and another one-fourth spent more than $161. The other half fell between the two figures.

Whatever your income, common sense dictates that you should never pay more than you can afford for a home. But by the same token, you should never be afraid to pay what you *can* afford.

Obviously, a family's size as well as other considerations may alter the generalizations about housing cost. A couple with no children, for example, does not have the same housing needs as a husband and wife with six children, all needing food, clothing, and eventually college educations. A childless couple, as a rule, will have more money available to buy and maintain a house than people who have the fixed and continuing expenses of a growing family. At the same time, the couple's housing needs are apt to be much less than a larger family.

Individual circumstances such as these can play havoc with all the rules. Two men may be making the same salary and even have the same amount of savings, yet one may be able to afford much more than the other.

Your pattern of living and the meaning a house has for you also can have something to do with how expensive a house you can afford. Let us look at two families to illustrate this point:

First, the Smiths. They are the stay-at-home type that likes to putter around the house and yard. Their hobbies are of the do-it-yourself kind. They lead a simple life, and the home is the center of their existence.

By contrast, the McDonalds enjoy taking long and expensive vacations every few years. Last year, they went to Hawaii. Next year they plan to go to Europe. They also like expensive clothes, and enjoy entertaining large groups.

It is obvious that the Smiths, with their less expensive life style, can afford to spend more for their home than the McDonalds.

As previously mentioned, if the lender will give you the mortgage you need, you can be reasonably certain that you are not going overboard. The lender's judgment is based on long years of experience—both his own experience and that of many others in the field.

Mortgage lenders have learned that the easy rules of thumb, like all formulas of this kind, contain a large measure of truth—but they are not the whole story.

For example, consider the case of Ed Jones. He is a rising young executive in a large industrial firm. The Jones family found the house they had been looking for, and they were certain they would have no trouble getting the $35,000 mortgage they needed. Ed was making $15,000 a year after taxes, and the $35,000 mortgage was less than the often-cited guideline that a family can spend 2½ times its annual income for a house.

But one lender after another refused to grant the mortgage. The reason? A credit check disclosed that Ed was over his head in debt. He had just bought a new car for himself, and another new one for his wife, both on the installment plan. With his country club expenses and other debts, and the cost of sending his son to college, there was not enough left over to pay the expenses of a new home. In the experienced judgment of the mortgage lenders, the Jones' were not a good credit risk.

Keep this point in mind: The lender will automatically make a credit check on you when you apply for a loan. So it is often advisable to defer the purchase of a new car, or other large installment purchases, until after you have bought your home.

RISING COST OF THE "TYPICAL" NEW HOUSE

	1965	Now
Sales price	$20,000	$27,000
Down payment	5,000	6,750
Monthly charges		
Mortgage payment	87.60	155.70
Property tax	26.75	39.70
Heat and utilities	24.85	29.55
Maintenance and repairs	11.05	14.00
Insurance	4.55	5.85
Total per month	154.80	244.80

In a little more than five years, the monthly outlay required to pay for the typical new house has gone up 58.3 percent. In the same period, the take-home pay of the average family has gone up only 34.4 percent. Result: Increasingly, families are finding it necessary to rent apartments instead of buying their own homes.

NOTE: The typical house built in 1965 contained 3 bedrooms, 2 baths and a total of 1,477 square feet of floor space. The typical house now contains 3½ bedrooms, 2½ baths, and 1,522 square feet of floor space.

Source: Estimates by USN&WR Economic Unit, based on data from Federal Housing Administration, U.S. Dept. of Commerce, U.S. Dept. of Housing and Urban Development.

Down payment: large or small?

The mortgage lender will finance the largest part of the cost of your home, but he will never finance all of it (except on some Veterans Administration loans). You will always need some cash when you buy a house, even if it is a low-priced one. And, of course, with expensive houses, the amount of cash required may be substantial.

The size of the down payment required will depend in large part on the type of loan you get. Most family money management counselors will encourage you to make as large a down payment as you can. The more you pay down, they say, the more you will save on interest costs, the lower your monthly mortgage payments will be, and

the more you will have for other things and for savings.
They add that the more you have invested in your house,
the better your credit standing will be, and the more you
can take out when you eventually sell. And finally, they
say, you should put as much down on the house as you
can because it is the best investment you can make for the
future.

There are, however, other factors to consider.

When you make a large down payment, you may find
later that you have more trouble selling your house. Suppose, for example, that you buy a $20,000 house with a
$5,000 down payment instead of only $2,000. A few years
later you want to sell. You have paid off $3,000 of your
original $15,000 mortgage, so—at the very least—you want to
find a buyer who can pay you $8,000 in cash and take over
the $12,000 mortgage. That sort of buyer may be hard
to find. For every buyer with $8,000 in cash available for a
down payment, there are many, many others who have a
smaller amount available—say $5,000 or less.

Factors the lender will evaluate

Let us suppose you have found the house you want.
You approach a lender to arrange a mortgage loan. What
factors will he evaluate in reaching his decision?

The answer will vary from lender to lender, but here
are three basic factors:

• Your effective income.
• Your debts and living costs.
• Your monthly housing expenses.

Let us examine these items in detail.

Your effective income. It must be dependable, continuing
income. If your income varies substantially from one year
to the next, it must be averaged out. The key word, in the
lender's eyes, is effective. That means take-home pay after
tax deductions and withholding taxes. It also rules out income that you will not get regularly, such as overtime pay,
annual bonuses, children's earnings, money from renting a
room, or income from occasional or part-time employment.

What about your wife's income? Does it count?

Yes—if her work has become an accepted part of your
family life. In other words, if you have married recently,

or if your wife has been working only a short time, her income probably will not be counted as part of the family's effective income. With young married couples, the wife's income also may be discounted on the theory she probably will be quitting work to have children.

Here is how one experienced mortgage lender handles the question of a second income:

If the wife is a professional, such as a school teacher, and is under the age of 32, this lender gives credit for half of her income. If she is over 32 and thus less likely to "retire" to motherhood, he allows full credit for her income. If the wife is in a nonprofessional occupation, this lender allows no credit for her income if she is under 32, half credit if she is 32 to 38, and full credit if she is older.

Your debts and living costs: These can be divided into two groups—living expenses and fixed obligations.

Living expenses include items such as food, clothing, insurance premiums, children's education, medical and dental care, transportation, recreation and entertainment, emergencies, and miscellaneous contributions to church and charity.

These living expenses vary from month to month—as anyone who has ever tried to balance a family's checkbook knows. One month there will be a big doctor's bill. Another month the insurance premiums will come due. The next month the children will all need back-to-school clothes.

To get a clearer picture of your living expenses, you might sort your cancelled checks and receipted bills into the previously mentioned categories (food, clothing, etc.). Do this for each month of the previous year, then add up the monthly totals for each category and divide by twelve. This will give you a monthly average for each of the living expenses categories.

Fixed obligations are easier to compute. They are regular, fixed installment payments for an automobile, appliances, or furniture (if purchased on time), as well as personal loans and other items such as support of elderly parents or regular payments into a savings or retirement fund.

Your monthly housing expenses: First, determine the monthly payments on the mortgage—principal and interest. Generally, these will be the same amount each month during the life of the mortgage; but in some cases, the payments will be slightly lower each year.

This table shows the monthly payments on a typical $10,000 mortgage, assuming an 8.5 percent interest rate:

Term of Mortgage	Monthly Payment
15 years	$98.50
20 years	86.80
25 years	80.60
30 years	76.90

For a $20,000 mortgage, these figures may be doubled; for larger or smaller amounts, they can be computed proportionately.

The figures shown in the table do not include taxes, insurance, utilities, maintenance, or miscellaneous costs. These sometimes are difficult to estimate, but some experts say you should allow at least one-half of 1 percent of the purchase price each year for maintenance. For a $20,000 house, this would mean budgeting about $100 a year for maintenance costs. Other authorities, however, contend this figure is too low. They say you should figure about 2 percent of the purchase price each year for maintenance and repairs. This would be $400 a year on a $20,000 house.

It is difficult to generalize about the costs of taxes and utilities. These costs vary widely, depending on a particular community's tax rate and upon the climate in different parts of the country. You can make inquiries of city or county officials to determine what the annual taxes would be. Friends who are homeowners can help you estimate the cost of utilities.

Miscellaneous expenses should be kept in mind. These include such items as garbage collection and lawn care. A garden could cost fifty dollars or more a year to keep up, with insecticides, fertilizer, and other supplies.

While you may be unable to make firm estimates on all of your maintenance costs, keep in mind that the upkeep of a house—even a new one—often costs more than you expect.

This was borne out in a survey a few years ago of 150 new homeowners in the metropolitan New York area. Seven out of ten of these interviewed said that the costs of maintaining their homes were greater than they had anticipated. Among the costs they listed as turning out to be higher than originally estimated were:

—Repairs and maintenance of lawn and grounds.
—Local and state taxes.
—Automobile and commuting expenses.
—Fuel costs for heating.
—Telephone bills.
—Heating and plumbing repairs.
—General house maintenance.
—Cost of appliances.
—Cost of entertainment.

This suggests that you should acquaint yourself in advance as realistically as you can with the expenses you will assume. Allow yourself a margin of error, but make certain that the margin is on the side of greater rather than lesser costs.

Extra costs to budget for

Some home buyers think they can transfer all of their possessions from one house to another without paying for anything but the moving. Unfortunately, it never seems to work that way. There are always things to buy for the new house. And they always seem to add up to more than you had planned to spend.

How much will it cost to outfit the new house?

The answer, of course, varies from family to family and house to house. But mortgage lenders say most people spend at least 10 percent of the cost of a home on such expenses as extra furniture, draperies, lighting fixtures, and kitchen equipment. This would be $1,000 or more for a $10,000 house, $2,000 or more for a $20,000 house, and so on.

A study made by university researchers several years ago seems to bear out this 10 percent formula. The survey covered 125 homeowners and disclosed that they spent an average of $1,600 on furniture and equipment in the first year—or roughly 10 percent of the average cost of the house. Today, with the average cost of a house at $36,000, the average for extras is $2,600, assuming the 10 percent formula.

Here are some tips on how to cope with these costs:

First, you should recognize that you are going to encounter these added expenses—no matter how firmly you resolve to avoid them.

Second, you should plan ahead and, at least to some degree, try to set some limits on the after-move expenses.

Third, try to stick to the 10 percent limit if it seems reasonable. Just because you have a limit will not mean that you will stay within it. But it does set a checkpoint and gives you a chance to retain some pocketbook control.

How should you pay for these after-the-move expenses?

Several methods are available. You can pay cash—if you have it. Or you can get a bank loan, or make the purchases on the installment plan. Or you can buy appliances and equipment as part of the mortgage loan.

It is best, of course, to pay cash. But if you cannot manage it, the next best method is to get a bank loan or use the installment plan. This way you will be paying for what you buy over a period that fits with its useful life. The third method, adding it to the mortgage loan, means you will be paying interest for years and years on the items you buy—in some cases long after they wear out.

Should you spend every cent?

When you have completed all of your calculations, you will have arrived at a figure that represents the most you can possibly spend for a house. The question then becomes: Should you go ahead and spend every last cent, or should you play it safe and spend a little less than your calculations show you can spend?

The answer, obviously, depends on the individual, his family situation, his personality, his way of managing his financial affairs. The American Bankers Association offers some suggestions which may help in making a decision.

It says you may wisely decide to commit every available cent to a home purchase if:

—You can make a large down payment which will immediately create a substantial equity in the property.

—You are buying a house that is not likely to require much spending for maintenance, repairs, and replacement for some years.

—You are willing and able to curb your spending on items subject to your control, such as new cars, vacations, or "luxuries."

—You are handy at making household repairs and doing maintenance jobs yourself.

—Your area's property taxes are low, and are likely to stay that way.

On the other hand, the Association suggests you probably should not go to the limit if:

—Property taxes are high in the area now, or if improvements like streets and schools are apt to push them up.

—You are in the habit of taking expensive vacations, or frequently financing new cars, appliances, boats, and the like, and you intend to keep on doing so.

—Your transportation or commuting costs will increase substantially when you move into a new house.

—You are buying a house that will require high maintenance outlays, or perhaps some remodeling.

—You do not have the time, talent, or inclination to tackle maintenance and repair jobs yourself.

—You need to build up reserves for some future expense, such as a child's college education; or you have unusual responsibilities or expenses, such as caring for elderly parents.

Hidden expenses

Newspapers are full of housing advertisements that say, "Total Price—No Extras." Nevertheless, there are hidden costs, and it is better to be aware of them beforehand, when you can plan and budget for them, than to be surprised by them later.

If you are buying a new house, you may face the prospect of putting in a lawn immediately upon moving in. Many developers now take care of planting the lawn and shrubs, including the costs in the price of the house.

But if you do not have this arrangement, you can figure on a minimum of $250 for a 50- by 100-foot lawn—if you are willing to buy with care and do the planting yourself.

For this $250 investment, you could get enough lawn seed, plus an assortment of low-growing evergreens, a half-dozen azaleas, a dozen rose bushes, a dozen or so perennials, several hundred flowering bulbs, and a couple of flowering trees.

You will also need a lawn mower, water hose, hoe, rake, spade, shears, and other tools. It will cost more, too, if you plant larger trees on your lot.

If you hire a landscape expert, figure on spending two or three times what you pay when you do it yourself. In other words, a $250 lawn would cost $500 to $750 if you hire someone, authorities say.

Among the most annoying hidden costs, especially in the case of those moving from an apartment, are the expenses of decorating the inside of a house. The chances are that the builder of a new subdivision house will decorate according to contract, rather than your wishes. This may mean, for example, that the wallpaper will not be of a design you like, or the paint used on the walls and ceiling will be of limited colors and quality.

It is relatively inexpensive, easy, and quick to repaint walls, and it is something you can do without a big investment in tools or time. Even the most inexperienced amateur can do this job successfully the first time. What will it cost? It depends on the size of your room, but one gallon of paint, costing from $3.50 to $7.00, will cover about 300 square feet. In other words, two gallons of paint should be enough to cover the walls of a 12- by 20-foot room. If you hire a professional paint contractor to do the job, he may charge $8.00 to $10.00 per 100 square feet.

Wallpapering is not as easy as painting, but it is a job you can tackle if you are reasonably handy. Modern wallpaper offers so many choices that you will probably spend considerable time shopping around before settling on the kind you want. The new vinyls are relatively expensive, but they offer a trouble-free surface for years to come. One roll of wallpaper, which costs anywhere from two

PRICES OF HOME SITES IN VARIOUS CITIES

Average Market Costs of New One-Family Lots

City	1960	1968	Percent Increase
Albany-Sch'y.-Troy, N.Y.	$1,494	$ 3,296	120.6%
Atlanta, Ga.	2,145	3,001	39.9
Baltimore, Md.	2,003	4,350	117.2
Baton Rouge, La.	2,904	3,125	7.6
Buffalo, N.Y.	2,218	3,329	50.1
Chicago, Ill.	3,346	3,821	14.2
Cincinnati, Ohio	3,289	4,207	27.9
Denver, Colo.	2,877	3,318	15.3
Des Moines, Iowa	2,489	3,457	38.9
Detroit, Mich.	2,711	3,477	28.3
Honolulu, Hawaii	6,575	13,502	105.4
Houston, Tex.	2,123	2,987	40.7
Kansas City, Mo.	2,488	3,001	20.6
Los Angeles-L.B., Calif.	4,122	8,276	100.8
Minneapolis-St. Paul, Minn.	2,173	3,816	75.6
Nashville, Tenn.	2,515	3,167	25.9
New Orleans, La.	3,673	4,974	35.4
New York, N.Y.	2,624	4,374	66.7
Omaha, Nebr.	2,303	3,107	34.9
Philadelphia, Pa.	2,202	3,912	77.7
Phoenix, Ariz.	2,112	3,529	67.1
Providence, R.I.	1,417	2,926	106.5
St. Louis, Mo.	2,844	3,477	22.3
Salt Lake City, Utah	2,072	3,089	49.1
San. Fran.-Oakland, Calif.	3,295	6,385	93.8
San Jose, Calif.	3,493	6,665	90.8
Seattle-Everett, Wash.	2,224	4,072	83.1
Washington, D.C.	2,943	5,319	80.7
Wilmington, Del.	2,417	3,274	35.5
Winston-Salem, N.C.	1,718	3,277	90.7

Source: FHA

dollars to thirty dollars, covers 30 square feet. If you have the job done by a professional, it will cost from twelve dollars to eighteen dollars per 100 square feet, plus the cost of the paper.

Many buyers of development homes discover there are other features which come with the house which are not what they want in terms of quality and appearance. For example, the lighting fixtures may be serviceable enough, but they may be the type intended more for utility than decoration. Similarly, the floor tiles may be of poor quality, devoid of interesting color or pattern. If you want more expensive tile, or a special color arrangement, you will have to pay extra.

Sometimes the builder will supply such accessories as storm windows and doors, screens, blinds, and the like. Inquiring in advance whether these items come with the house may avert misunderstandings and disappointments later.

The same inquiries should be made concerning appliances. The fact that a particular set of appliances was installed in the model house you inspected does not mean that you are going to get any or all of them, or that you will even get the same brand or model. Of course, this bleak picture is far from uniform. Some builders, particularly those with pride in their work and reputation, provide more adequate appliances. But it is wise to be warned in advance so you will be on your guard.

There are still other potential hidden costs.

Your old draperies, curtains, blinds, rugs, and carpets may be in good shape, but it is unlikely they will precisely fit the new windows and floors. Costly alterations may be necessary.

Some of your furniture, particularly built-to-order pieces, may not be adaptable to the new house. And you may want built-ins made for the new house—bookcases, for example.

You may have agreed to buy furniture, draperies, blinds, garden equipment, and other items from the previous owner. But make certain you know ahead of time whether the cost is included in the purchase price of the house. You also may have assumed that some items—lighting fixtures or cabinets, for example—went with the house, only to discover on arrival that the previous owner has removed them. You may want to make immediate repairs to the fence, if one comes with the house. Or, if zoning regulations permit, you may want to put up a fence. In either case, it will cost money.

There may be other expenses you never dreamed of. You may be required, for example, to pay for your own trash removal, an item which may have been a municipal service where you previously lived. Or you may be obligated to join a neighborhood improvement association with steep annual dues.

Some of these items may be more annoying than costly, but a wise buyer will anticipate all hidden costs so as to avoid unpleasant surprises after moving into a new home.

How to Pick the Right House in the Right Place

In the view of many experts, location is the single most important factor to consider when you buy a house. This is especially true if you are likely to move again, because location can mean a big plus in resale value. But profit considerations aside, the happiness of your family may depend on your choice of community and neighborhood. When you buy a house, you are buying more than just a piece of land and a building. You are acquiring neighbors, a neighborhood and a community. The wrong choice can make you miserable—and ruin your investment.

There are a number of points to consider in selecting a location.

As you drive or walk around the neighborhood, look to see if the houses are well maintained, the yards neatly trimmed and the sidewalks and streets clean. If the houses are poorly maintained and if yards are littered and unkept, the chances are that the neighborhood is deteriorating. This should not automatically rule out the neighborhood. Look for signs of revitalization, such as homes being remodeled. If the neighborhood is on its way back, you might be able to find a bargain in a fine old house that needs a little work to restore it.

As you inspect the neighborhood, notice how far the houses are from the street. The neighborhood is more attractive if they are well back from the street. However, this can be a mixed blessing. It means most of your land is in front, where it is on display, instead of in back, where it can make living more pleasant.

The neighborhood will be more attractive, too, if there are large trees. In many new developments, builders make every effort to save as many mature trees as they can. They have learned that trees add to the sales appeal of a house.

The style and price range of other houses in the immediate neighborhood should be considered. Some people dislike the monotony of a neighborhood with block after block of look-alike houses. Yet, on the other hand, a neighborhood that is a hodgepodge of different styles, sizes and price ranges can create problems. For instance, houses in a group seem to gravitate toward one another in value. This happens no matter how well built one is and how poorly built the one next to it is. Experts say a street seems automatically to put a price tag on every other house, averaging them out. That is why they offer this advice: Do not build a $40,000 house in a block of $15,000 houses. The ideal neighborhood is one which offers enough variety to complement the right degree of similarity. That ideal neighborhood may be hard to find, but keep this point in mind: You are apt to be happier in a neighborhood where most of the people are not much better off nor worse off than you economically. Chances are most of them will share some of your tastes and interests. If you move into a neighborhood where everyone makes two or three times as much as you do, you may find yourself struggling to keep up with your neighbors.

Another key aspect is the physical layout of the neighborhood. Curved streets are preferable to straight streets. The curving cuts down on the amount of traffic and the speed at which it flows. This means the streets are safer for children. Good physical planning also eliminates as many four-way intersections as possible. And if there are cul-de-sacs, a good plan allows plenty of room for turn-arounds. While it is best that your home be accessible to a major traffic artery, such as an expressway, the artery should be far enough away so that it creates neither a noise nor a safety problem. If the neighborhood is hilly, the streets should be laid out so that they rise gradually. Sudden or steep rises can create driving problems in bad weather.

Another major consideration is the location of the home in relation to your place of employment, to shopping and recreation facilities, churches, and hospitals. In most cases, distances should be measured in terms of minutes, rather than miles. For example, it is all but meaningless to be told that the house is ten miles from downtown. That ten-mile trip could take twenty minutes to drive, or it could take sixty minutes. It is best not to take another's word for commuting time. Make the trip yourself at the time of day you will be making the daily trip. Even if you plan to drive to and from work, it is a good idea to determine what kind of public transportation is available. Find out the fares, check schedules to see if trains or buses make frequent runs and maintain service at night. This can be important if you have guests who do not drive and depend on public transportation.

It is best, by one rule of thumb, to have local shopping facilities—such as a supermarket and drug store—within one mile of home. And, ideally, a major shopping area—such as a regional shopping center—should be within ten miles.

As for recreational facilities, it is best if a playground or park is nearby, especially if you have children. And you should check the availability of other facilities, such as a golf course, swimming pool, tennis courts, movies, and libraries. If you plan to be active in church, check to see whether one of your choice is conveniently located.

The local school situation obviously is important to every home-buyer with school-age children. The buyer who does not have school-age children will be paying school taxes in any event, and he may want to sell his house later to someone with children.

Families naturally want schools within walking distance of home. Children should not have to cross any heavily traveled street on their way to school. If schools are not within walking distance, you will want to check school bus routes.

If possible, you should visit the school and talk to the principal and teachers. Find out whether the school operates on double sessions. If it does, this is an indication of overcrowding. Visit the classrooms. Are they clean and well-lighted? Are books and equipment up-to-date and well cared for? Are there special rooms for art and science? Does the school have a library? A gymnasium?

It is difficult to determine, with a short visit, the quality of education available in the school. But you can call the local school superintendent and ask how much money is spent per pupil. How does this compare with other school systems in the area? As a general rule, the more money spent usually means the system pays teachers better salaries, and thus is able to attract better-qualified teachers. You might also try to find out the school's educational standing from someone in the educational field.

If you plan to send your children to private or parochial schools, you should make the same checks as you would for public schools.

In addition to schools, you should inquire about municipal services. Is police protection adequate and effective? How far away is the fire station, and is it staffed with well-trained, full-time firemen or part-time volunteers? What about garbage and trash removal—is it provided by the local government or do you have to arrange for private collection? Is the house already equipped with all utilities —water, electricity, gas, storm and sanitary sewers?

You may have to visit city hall to get answers to some of these questions. While you are there, you should seek out the zoning commission's office and study the zoning map for the area you are considering. Look for areas which are set aside for business and industry, parks and schools, apartment buildings, and single family homes. Try to determine how these zoning rules will hurt or help the property values in your area. Bear in mind that zoning regulations relate to the future. What has been done in the past may not conform to future zoning. For example, you may find existing two-family homes in an area now zoned for single family homes.

Although zoning regulations can be changed, they give you some idea of what the neighborhood may be like in the future. This brings up an important point. As you look at different areas, you might keep asking yourself: What will this neighborhood be like five years from now? Ten years from now? Twenty years from now?

Zoning regulations, as we noted, can provide some clues. So can the city's pattern of growth. For instance, if a city's most fashionable neighborhood is now in the southeast section, growth in that direction is apt to consist of higher quality homes. If the less desirable section of town is the northwest part, areas beyond it are likely to be lower-quality homes. There are some exceptions to these broad generalities, but housing experts say it usually is best to pick a location that is in the same general area of the city's more desirable neighborhoods.

With these pointers on finding the best location in mind, let us consider other important questions. What type house should you buy? Old or new? Ready-built or custom-built?

The custom-built house

The dream of many American families is to have an architect-designed, custom-built home. But most families never realize this dream. The main reason: Custom-built homes generally are high priced. Only a lucky few can afford them.

There are some exceptions, of course. Some families who are determined to have a one-of-a-kind house that suits their needs are able to get it. If you feel the urge to become one of these families, you should know the advantages and disadvantages of custom building.

You should be aware, for example, that it takes a long time to have a house built from personalized plans. Six months to a year—sometimes longer—is not uncommon.

And you should know that your initial investment with a custom-built house may be three to four times more than normally required as down payment on many moderate-priced homes. An illustration: For a typical $20,000 house in a subdivision, you might pay out $2,000 in initial costs, including the down payment. If you have a $20,000

This striking house, custom-built for jazz pianist Dave Brubeck, is perched on a peak of the hills around Oakland, California.

house custom-built, the initial costs are apt to be $7,000 to $8,000.

You almost always need to own your lot free and clear before you move ahead with your plans to build—and land costs have soared in recent years. For instance, the average price of a building lot financed by FHA in 1950 was $1,035, according to a government survey. In 1969 the average price was $4,300—a four-fold increase in less than two decades.

Experts say you should surpress any urge to draw your own house plans—unless, of course, you happen to be an architect or designer by profession. Unless you have the skills, you may end up with a dreadful mess instead of a dream home.

The ideal way of getting your house plans is to hire an architect. The architect can give you expert advice on how to get the most space for your money, and how to select the right materials. He can even handle details like getting bids from contractors and supervising their work to make certain the house is built the way you want it. Most important, the architect can design for you a house that fits your family's tastes, interests, and needs.

Why, then, does not everyone who builds a new house seek out an architect's services? One reason is that the average individual fears that the architect will charge a high fee. Actually, the architect's fee usually is a percentage of the cost of the house to be built. The fee generally ranges anywhere from 8 percent to 15 percent, depending on the particular job. But a good architect may be able to save you enough, through skillful design and the right selection of materials, to cover part of his fee.

Some architects are reluctant to accept the job of designing a small, fairly inexpensive house. The reason is that it takes almost as much time to design a $20,000 house as it does, say, a $60,000 house. With a 15 percent fee, the architect would receive $3,000 on the $20,000 house—which might not be enough to pay his office overhead and other expenses. And architects say they can make more money designing big office buildings and shopping centers than designing houses. So you may have trouble locating an architect willing to take on the job.

One way to find him is to talk to contractors, lenders, and real estate people. Once you locate an architect, the first step is to outline, as concisely as you can, what you want in the house. The architect needs to know as much as possible about your family's living habits, tastes, and desires. When he has all this information in hand, he will make preliminary drawings. He will submit these to you for your suggestions, criticism, and further ideas. Next, the architect will prepare working plans and a list of materials and specifications. These will go to contractors for bids. Once that is done, work can start on the house itself.

If you do not want to hire an architect, there still is a way to obtain the advantages of professional design. This can be done with "stock plans," which are sets of professionally prepared drawings that you can order by mail. For twenty-five dollars to fifty dollars, you can get a set of blueprints, a list of materials, and a specifications sheet on which contractors can base bids. You may have seen references to such plans in magazines. They also are available through building materials dealers and other outlets.

The detailed working drawings which you order show floor plans, dimensions, structural details, and illustrations of how the house will look from each side. Usually, these plans are drawn to conform to FHA standards, which indicate acceptable standards of design and construction but do not automatically insure a superior house.

Before you set out to build a house from stock plans, you should make certain that it will conform to local building codes and zoning regulations. Keep in mind, too, that you will have to follow the plans without substantial changes—so you will want to pick a plan that fits your family's actual needs. And, by all means, make certain that the house can be built for the amount of money you have to spend.

Whichever route you follow—stock plans or architect's drawings—you will need to hire a contractor to build the house. He takes the plans and oversees construction from the moment ground is broken until the moment you move in. He acts as a sort of manager of the project, buying the material, hiring the workmen, and obtaining the necessary permits. Much of the actual work—like plumbing, wiring, painting, and roofing—will be done by subcontractors selected by the general contractor.

How do you select a good contractor? The most important consideration is whether the contractor is completely reputable and responsible. Check with your local Chamber of Commerce and Better Business Bureau, or consult several local banks or real estate agents. You can obtain the name of other homeowners he has worked for, and find out whether they have been satified with his work.

Once you have checked the qualifications of several contractors, you can ask them to submit competitive bids for the job. You will have to supply them with the floor plan and list of specifications, and give them a reasonable length of time to submit their bids. When the bids are in, you may discover that the contractors have proposed some changes, perhaps in the type and quality of materials. This means you will have to analyze the bids carefully before selecting one.

The two most common types of agreements with contractors are:

- Cost-plus. Under this type of agreement, you pay all the costs of construction, plus either a stated dollar fee or a percentage of the total costs, such as 10 or 15 percent.

- Lump sum. With this type of arrangement, the contractor agrees to build the house as described in the plans and specifications for a stated amount. This sum includes all his costs and profits.

The obvious disadvantage of the percentage cost-plus arrangement is that the contractor might be tempted to let costs spiral, since the higher the costs the higher his fee. But with the lump sum contract, a builder might be tempted to cut corners on materials or workmanship in an effort to make a larger profit. Such instances may be rare, but they underscore the importance of carefully checking the reputation of the contractor beforehand.

Generally, the contractor wants to have his money in stages—a portion when the foundation is laid, more when the outside structure is completed, another portion when the interior is done. You should, however, make certain you inspect the job at different stages, especially before the final payment is made.

There are several other points which should be covered in any agreement with a contractor. For instance, it should include a statement that the contractor is responsible for paying all subcontractors; that he will pay for liability and workmen's compensation insurance; and that he will abide by local building ordinances. In addition, it is wise to obtain a surety bond. This is your insurance that the job will be completed, as agreed. If something happens to the contractor, the company issuing the surety bond will see that the job is finished.

Buying a new, ready-built house

It is clear that a custom-built house will involve you in very many details. And, as noted earlier, it most likely will be more expensive. It is for such reasons that most people buy ready-built homes, either new ones or older, previously occupied ones.

Ready-built houses are generally less expensive because they are the product of professional builders who, by using the latest large-scale methods, are able to achieve economies not possible on a small-scale, one-at-a-time basis. The tract builder is likely to buy at one swoop enough land for a 100-acre subdivision. He contracts for materials in huge quantities, thus getting lower prices. He is apt to have his own specialized construction crews, eliminating the need for subcontractors. By using the latest land planning techniques, he is able to get more homes per acre yet still have room for parks and open spaces. And by arranging financing ahead of time, he may be able to offer you savings in interest charges. This can be very important at a time of high interest rates and tight money. In short, the tract builder usually is able to build more houses at lower cost.

One drawback, in the view of some, is that tract houses are designed and built for the "typical" family. The question, of course, is this: What is a typical family? Is it the family with one child and two cars? Or four children and one car? Is it a family with $12,000 a year income? Or with $20,000 a year income?

The tract builder usually offers a variety of models. One of them may suit your needs, but be prepared to compromise if you want to take advantage of the economies of multiple production housing.

In many ways, judging a brand new house is more difficult than judging an older one. In the first place, you probably will have to base your decision on the inspection of a model house, not the house you are buying. Keep in mind that the builder will have taken pains to make the model house perfect in every respect. It will be on a good lot and will be handsomely landscaped. It will be loaded with all the optional extras—like intercom and central vacuum system—and it is likely to be outfitted with small scale furniture to make the rooms look larger. The appliances in the model house are likely to be of better quality than normally furnished.

While the model home may be loaded with extras, there is one thing that cannot be tampered with: the basic floor plan. After you have been house-hunting for a while, you will be able to size up a floor plan and quickly determine whether it is good or bad. The following may be helpful to a novice:

The house should have three well-defined zones. One is the noisy work and play zone (mother's kitchen, father's workshop, and children's play area). The second is the formal living and dining area. The third is the secluded bedroom and bath zone. There should be "buffers" between these zones. This usually should be something more than an ordinary interior wall. The buffer might, for example, be closets back-to-back.

The house also should have a good traffic pattern. The different zones and different rooms should be located so as to allow easy movement between them. Here is one way to check out a traffic pattern: On the floor plan, draw lines from the front door to all other rooms in the house, following the route you would be likely to take if you actually were in the house. Do the same from the back door to all other rooms. Now draw lines from each bedroom to the nearest bath. And draw lines from the kitchen to the living room, dining room, bedrooms, and bathroom. Now look at the lines you have drawn. They represent "traffic corridors." Ideally, the living room should be a "dead end"—a calm, relaxed room without a lot of traffic.

You should also examine the floor plan with an eye toward storage space. Are there ample closets in the bedrooms? Is there a closet near the main entrance for coats and hats? What about storage space for items such as the ironing board, bathroom linen, laundry detergent, tools, luggage, sports and outdoor equipment? By one rule of thumb, you will need at least 30 square feet of general inside storage space. Other experts say 50 square feet would be better. To help you get a clearer idea of how much storage space is included in the house, you might shade in the closets and storage areas on the floor plan.

This will aid you, too, in the next step: determining how much of the house is useable as living space. The closets and storage areas which you shaded are not useable living space. Neither are the traffic corridors you marked earlier. And, for that matter, neither are the floor areas which must be kept clear to allow doors to open. You might shade these areas, too. What is left is your living space. Is it large enough? Or, more importantly, will the living space accommodate the furniture you intend to use, and still leave enough room to move about?

By following these steps, you will be able to analyze any floor plan, and separate the good from the bad.

It is more difficult to tell good construction from bad, but you should make the effort.

Outside the house, you should make certain that proper grading and drainage carry run-off water away from the house. And if the lot has not been landscaped, check the soil to see if it will take plantings, or whether top soil will have to be brought in.

The gutters to carry rain water off the roof should be of a type that will not rust easily. If the lot's drainage is good, the absence of gutters is not necessarily a defect. But if the drainage is bad, gutters are a must.

If the exterior walls are brick or other masonry, you can test the quality of the cementing material by digging a penknife into it. If the mortar crumbles to the touch, poor material probably has been used. And while you are checking the masonry walls, make certain there is caulking between the windows and door frames and the walls.

Check the foundations, both inside and outside, if possible. Small cracks may be the result of natural settling and do not necessarily affect the structural soundness of the house. But long, deep cracks in the foundation may be a sign of uneven settling. They could be a danger signal. Authorities say if you see any cracks at all, it is best to consult an expert to determine if they are serious.

Inside the house, look for cracking or buckling of wallboard. It may be only a sign of the normal shrinkage or settling of a new house, but it could be an indication of poor construction. For example, if green lumber is used, nails can pop loose and cause wallboard to bulge or buckle.

Wood panelings and moldings should be inspected closely. Cracks or gashes could be an indication of inferior lumber. And make certain that baseboards meet the floor snugly. A gap here might be another indication of green lumber, or poor workmanship. Check, too, for any rough spots in the woodwork, perhaps knots which show through the paint. This again may mean that inferior lumber has been used.

No matter how new the house, floors should not creak when you put your weight on them. Creaking can indicate the builder has used poor lumber, or employed poor construction practices.

You should also inspect the plumbing, electrical wiring, and heating systems. Copper or brass water pipes usually are considered superior, since they will not rust. Even if there is no air conditioning, wiring should be adequate to carry such a heavy load. This is better done when a house is built, rather than having to rewire later. Modern electrical systems make use of circuit breaker boxes, instead of the old-fashioned fuse box. As for electrical outlets, by one rule of thumb every wall three feet long or longer should have at least one double outlet. If the wall measures more than 15 feet, there should be two outlets. Make certain there are enough outlets for all the kitchen appliances—toaster, blender, electric fry pan, and the like. And check the location of the light switches. They should be conveniently positioned near the entrance of every room. The heating system should be inspected to make certain all rooms are heated evenly and quickly. If you expect to convert a portion of the basement into a game room, or add a bedroom in the attic, you should determine whether the furnace is capable of heating such additions.

These tips will help you when you look at new houses. But what about older houses?

Buying an older house

There is an emotional appeal which often leads people to buy a charming older house which later turns out to be more expensive than anticipated. The costs of repairs and improvements must be weighed against the advantages of older houses.

The following considerations may be helpful:

Space: If you have a large or growing family, an older house may give you more living space and more rooms than a new home in the same price range. The rooms are apt to be larger, too. And you are likely to get an ample attic, more bulk storage space and a full dining room—rather than a dining alcove. But you may find yourself with an undersized garage, no family room and small, or too few, closets.

Extras: When you buy an older house, you often pick up a bonus in carpeting and draperies that may come as part of your purchase price. Do not overlook the big savings, too, in an older house's mature shrubs, trees, and lawn. Even a smaller five-year-old house is apt to have $300 or more worth of plantings. Compare these with the minimum costs of landscaping a new subdivision home.

Location: Older neighborhoods generally offer handy access to downtown shopping and places of employment. But make certain the house is not located on a rush-hour artery which could be hazardous for children walking to and from school—or for getting out of the driveway. If the house is situated on a quiet side street and is convenient to present or projected freeways, the location itself will increase its value. Be sure to inspect the general appearance of other houses in the neighborhood. If yards are unkempt or if peeling paint is predominent, you may be viewing a blighted neighborhood in the making. And you should, of course, make a point to check out the school district.

Taxes: Chances are you will pay lower property taxes on an older house than a new one of similar size and price. In some cases, the taxes may be as much as one third less. As a general rule, the older the house, the lower the assessment. Original assessments of twenty to thirty years ago probably have been raised, but not in line with newer construction. In some communities, however, reassessment programs have been conducted, sharply increasing the taxes on older houses.

Property taxes tend to be stable in a settled built-up neighborhood. This obviously is an advantage over new areas, where the tax rate may skyrocket because new schools, streets, sewers, and other facilities are being built.

If you are thinking of buying an older house, it may be advisable to check with the town or county clerk or appraiser to see if your purchase price could substantially affect the assessment. In areas where market value is a big factor, your price could mean a big increase in the assessed value—and a tax rise.

Maintenance: There is no simple method of computing maintenance costs for older homes. Costs vary widely from house to house and from area to area. Experts say that after you have renovated a ten-year-old house and moved in, subsequent maintenance costs should be about the same as for a new house of the same construction.

These experts offer other general guidelines:

An older house may have limited or inferior insulation, so that costs of heating could be higher.

Outside, the upkeep on an unpainted brick or stone house will be cheaper than for a frame, stucco, or painted brick house.

A frame exterior also may require new siding.

There is always a chance that the roof will need repair.

Inside, much depends on how well the house has been kept up.

Houses built twenty or thirty years ago are generally of different, heavier construction. The walls, for example, are usually plaster, not dry wall.

Obviously, the older the house, the sooner you will have to replace plumbing pipes, furnace, inadequate wiring, or kitchen appliances.

A house that is, say, five to ten years old, may be free of all "new house bugs." But you might be wise to seek professional help in checking the furnace, plumbing, and such structural features as foundation walls, columns, and girders. Home inspection services usually cost from $35 to $200, depending on the value of the house, but they could be a sound investment.

Repairs: The cost of repairs may be taken into account when negotiating the price of an older house. For example, if a new roof will soon be needed, establish the cost that will be involved, and add this to get the total price you actually will be paying for the house. Or, if you feel the price is already high, you might offer the owner less, deducting the cost of a new roof.

Financing: This could be a big factor in your decision. Sizeable savings are possible if you can take over the existing mortgage.

Problems of money and mortgages are examined in the next chapter.

What You Should Know About Money and Mortgages

Buying a home is no simple transaction. It is not like buying a new coat, which may take a few minutes, or like buying a new car, which may take a few hours. Buying a home is much more complex. It may take weeks to complete the transaction. Many legal technicalities are involved, and a good deal of money.

Even though a house is likely to be the largest single purchase they ever make, many families dive into home-ownership without knowing the fundamentals of such important matters as purchase contracts, mortgages, and closing costs.

The following simplified, step-by-step treatment of many complicated aspects of buying a home may help you avoid potentially costly pitfalls.

The purchase contract

When you have made up your mind to buy a particular house and have reached agreement with the seller on a price, a contract of sale must be signed. This document also is known as a "binder," "purchase contract," "purchase agreement," or "deposit receipt." It is signed by both the purchaser and the seller.

The contract of sale is important because it assures you that you will get the house at the agreed upon price. It gives you time to work out details like checking the title and arranging the financing. But you should remember that the contract binds you to go through with the deal, if the seller lives up to the contract provisions.

Customarily, when you sign a contract, you are required to make a deposit. The size of the deposit varies. In some instances it can range up to 10 percent of the price of the house. Generally, this deposit is either returned when the actual transaction takes place or is applied to the down payment or closing costs.

Before you sign a contract of sale, make sure you understand all of its provisions. Since the contract is a legal document containing legal terms which are hard for the average person to understand, it is advisable to hire an attorney before you sign it. The best way to protect yourself from possible pitfalls is to get competent advice from a lawyer who is familiar with the real estate practices in your area.

The Veterans Administration, in its "Guide for Veterans Planning to Buy or Build Homes With a GI Loan," says your sales contract should cover the following points:

—The sales price should be specified in the contract. For your protection, it usually is best if the contract states that the sales price is not subject to change. Some contracts contain a so-called "escalator" clause which permits the builder of a new house to increase the price because of future cost increases. A contract without an "escalator" clause may be the best from your point of view, but for many reasons the builder may not be willing to build without such a clause. If the builder insists upon such a clause you should recognize that it will give him the right to increase the price to you subject to whatever conditions may be stated in your contract.

—The sales contract should state the amount of cash payment required from you and the manner of financing the balance. If the contract says that you must arrange the loan for the balance due, it should provide that any cash deposit you make will be refunded to you if you cannot obtain a loan within a stated period of time.

—The sales contract should include an itemized list of anticipated closing costs and prepaid items with an understanding as to who is to pay each. This may enable you to determine how much cash you will need at closing and may avert disputes.

—The contract should require the seller to convey the property to you on or before an agreed date. The contract should set forth your right to withdraw and recover your deposit if the property is not conveyed on time.

—In the case of new construction, the contract should provide that the builder will complete the home in accordance with definite plans and specifications by a specified date or within a reasonable time thereafter. The plans and specifications describe the type of house that will be built, the dimensions, the type of material to be used, and other details.

—Before you sign the contract you should review the plans and specifications to which the contract refers, or have someone do it for you. The average person is not ordinarily able to read the meaning of a set of plans and specifications or to determine their adequacy, or to judge later whether the actual construction is being done in accordance with those plans and specifications. Before you sign the contract you would do well to have some trained person review the plans and specifications for you. You may find that you or the builder will want to make a change or two in the original plans and specifications as the building progresses. Those are matters to be arranged between the builder and you, although the lender may require that the changes be submitted for approval.

—The contract should contain a provision determining who will be responsible for the property from the date of the contract to the date when the house is conveyed to you. The builder or seller usually takes this responsibility.

—You should not sign any contract containing a so-called "safety" or "escape" clause which would enable the builder or seller to back out of the contract any time he wants—unless you as the buyer also have similar rights.

—The contract should clearly identify any easily removable or built-in equipment, appliances or other items, which are to be included in the transaction.

It should be stressed again that these are just some of the things that a prospective homeowner should be careful about in signing his sales contract. Legal documents are often complicated. There is no substitute for competent advice from a lawyer.

Financing a house

Few families are able to pay cash for their homes. The vast majority borrows a large sum of money from a mortgage lender, thus reducing the amount of cash required to buy a home. The mortgage money itself comes from a vast, nationwide pool of capital formed by savings—money put aside by bank depositors, savings and loan association shareholders, the payers of insurance premiums, and the contributors to pension funds. Without the mortgage lender's ability to dip into this pool for long-term loans, there would be few sales of older houses, and few new houses would be built.

From a legal standpoint, the mortgage is a lender's security that you, the buyer, will live up to your pledge to repay the loan. The lender is known as the "mortgagee." You, the buyer, are known as the "mortgagor."

The mortgage loan is somewhat similar to other types of loans. For example, when you buy an automobile on credit, you sign a sales contract agreeing that the automobile dealer or the finance company or the bank will retain legal title to the car until you have paid off the loan. Then the title is transferred to you. The car itself served as security for the loan. You also use your home as security when you obtain a mortgage. The mortgage papers you sign will specify that if you fail to meet the repayment schedule, the lender will bring a foreclosure suit to recover the loan.

There is one big difference between the automobile loan and the mortgage loan—the way in which interest is calculated. Here is an illustration:

Henry Murray borrowed $2,000 from his bank a few years ago to buy a new car. At that time, interest rates were lower, so he was able to get a 5 percent rate and a three-year repayment period. His monthly payments were $65.36, so he repaid a total of $2,353. The financing costs amounted to $353. Now if that had been a $2,000 mortgage loan, instead of an automobile loan, he would have had to repay only $2,159 in three years—or a difference of $194.

The reason for the difference is this: On the car loan, the bank immediately discounted the interest for three years in advance. In other words, to get $2,000 he had to borrow $2,353. Then, in addition, the bank charged interest not on the $2,000 he actually received, but on the $2,353 which he borrowed. In contrast, with a mortgage loan, interest is calculated only on the unpaid balance due.

In the depression of the 1930s, many families lost their homes because they were unable to make their mortgage payments. But mortgages in those days were different from the ones of today. Then, it was common to have "straight term" mortgages. With this type, there would be a level payment of interest for a period of years, then the entire mortgage would come due on a certain future date. If, on the due date, the entire balance was not paid, the homeowner would face foreclosure proceedings.

Today, however, most mortgages are of the constant payment, self-liquidating type, known technically as amortized loans. With these mortgages, the payments are the same each month over the years. A portion of each payment goes to pay the interest, and a portion goes to retire the principal, so that when the final payment is made you own the house free and clear. There is no massive payment as in the "straight term" mortgages of the 1930s.

The amount of the monthly payment which goes to pay interest gets smaller as the principal is reduced. This is because the interest is calculated on the unpaid balance due. For example, if you owe $15,000 on the mortgage that still has seventeen years to run, you have to pay interest on the use of the $15,000 for seventeen years. But when you make one of your monthly payments and reduce the principal by, say, $75, then the next month you would owe interest on $14,925 for sixteen years and eleven months. The total monthly payment remains the same, but the proportion of interest and principal are different each month. For instance, let us look at a $10,000,

WHAT YOU MUST PAY
FOR $25,000 MORTGAGE

Four Repayment Terms at 8 Percent Interest

Term	Monthly	Yearly	Total for Term
15 years	$239	$2,868	$43,020
20 years	209	2,511	50,220
25 years	193	2,316	57,900
30 years	183.50	2,202	66,060

twenty-year 6 percent mortgage. Of the first $72 monthly payment, $50 goes for interest and about $22 goes to retire the principal. But ten years later, $32 of the monthly payment is for interest and $40 is for the principal. And by the seventeenth year, only $12 goes for interest. The other $60 is applied to the principal.

As the principal is reduced over the years, there is a corresponding increase in your equity—in other words, the portion of the value of the house that belongs to you, free of debt. If the house remains as valuable as it was at the time you bought it, your equity equals the amount of your down payment, plus the principal you have paid back, plus the value of any permanent improvements you might have made. If the house increases in value, your equity will grow even faster.

Where do you go to get a mortgage loan? The usual places are banks, savings and loan associations, insurance companies, and mortgage bankers. These lenders' operations differ somewhat, but the loans they make usually fall into three categories—VA, FHA, and conventional.

VA loans

Veterans Administration loans, also called GI loans, are

guaranteed by the Veterans Administration. In other words, a lending institution makes the loan to the qualified veteran, and the Veterans Administration enters into an agreement with the lender to guarantee or insure a loan up to a certain amount. This means the lender will probably not suffer any loss in the event the homeowner fails to repay the loan.

From the borrower's point of view, one of the most attractive features of a VA loan is that it permits the purchase of a home with little or no down payment. Other advantages include a generally low rate of interest, a long period of amortization, and property appraisal by the VA based on the rule of reasonable value. The last provision has kept many veterans from purchasing a poorly constructed home or paying a greatly inflated priced.

Since the Veterans Administration started guaranteeing loans in 1944, more than 7.5 million veterans obtained mortgages totaling nearly $75 billion. There have been wide fluctuations in VA-guaranteed mortgage lending volume. In 1955, for instance, a record $7.3 billion volume was recorded. But in 1961, volume dipped to a low of $1.8 billion. In 1969, it stood at $4.1 billion.

The fluctuation can be traced in part to congressional action amending the original loan guarantee program, mainly to extend eligibility under the program. A veteran may use his entitlement up to ten years from the date of his discharge, plus an additional year for each three months of wartime service. The cutoff date for the eligibility of World War II veterans is July 25, 1970; for Korean War veterans, January 31, 1975.

In 1966, Congress passed the so-called "Cold War GI Bill" and extended the VA loan guarantee program to veterans who were on active duty at least 181 days since January 31, 1955. These post-Korean veterans have twenty years from their date of discharge to apply for a VA guaranteed loan.

In addition to veterans, men still in the armed service who have at least two years active duty are eligible for Veterans Administration guaranteed loans. So are unremarried widows of men who died as the result of service in World War II or the Korean War.

The Veterans Administration makes no charge for guaranteeing or insuring a loan for a World War II or Korean conflict veteran. "Cold war" veterans must pay a fee of one-half of 1 percent of the amount of the loan. For example, if the loan amount is $16,000, the fee would be $80. This fee, which may be included in the loan, is remitted to the Veterans Administration by the lender.

Under the program, loans up to 100 percent of the VA appraised value for periods up to thirty years are available at an interest rate specified by the government. In early 1970, the maximum interest allowed was 8½ percent. There is no maximum amount for such a loan. However, 100 percent Veterans Administration loans on homes which cost more than $25,000 are exceptional because the Veterans Administration guarantees only 60 percent of a loan up to a maximum of $12,500. Consequently, loans exceeding $25,000 involve a higher risk for the lender.

Veterans who had used their right to obtain a mortgage before May 7, 1968, still are eligible for at least a $5,000 guarantee. This should be enough for a no-down payment loan up to $25,000. The reason many veterans get a "second chance" to use the Veterans Administration program is that on May 7, 1968, the amount of the Veterans Administration guarantee for home loans was changed from $7,500 to $12,500. The amount of the guarantee to which the veteran is entitled comes to $12,500 less the amount he used on prior loans. The precise amount remaining in each case will be calculated by the lender, or, on request, by the Veterans Administration.

In addition to guaranteeing home mortgages, the VA makes direct government loans to veterans who live in "housing credit shortage areas"—generally rural areas and small towns where GI loans from private institutions have not been and are not now available. The maximum loan amount available generally is $17,500.

FHA loans

FHA mortgage loans are insured by the Federal Housing Administration to protect lenders from losses in case owners fail to pay. Under the FHA program, the home buyer makes a small down payment and obtains a mortgage for the rest of the purchase price. The mortgage loan is made by a bank, savings and loan association, mortgage company, insurance company, or other FHA-approved lender. It is not a government loan—the FHA does not lend money or build homes. Because FHA mortgage insurance protects the lender against loss on the mortgage, the lender can allow more liberal mortgage terms than the home buyer might otherwise be able to afford. Generally, FHA-insured loans have a lower down payment and longer maturity than conventional loans.

The Federal Housing Administration was created by the National Housing Act of 1934 and operates various loan insurance programs. By far the most common type of mortgages insured by FHA comes under Section 203 (b). Since 1934, about $88 billion in mortgages have been written under this section of the law. Fifty-five billion dollars are currently in force as of the end of 1969.

To qualify for an FHA-insured loan, the property must meet FHA minimum standards. These require, in general, that the house be livable, soundly built, and suitably located as to site and neighborhood. The individual seeking an FHA-insured loan must have a good credit rating, the cash needed at closing of the mortgage, and enough steady income to make the mortgage payments without difficulty. FHA sets no upper age limit for a borrower. Nor does it say he must have a certain income to buy a home at a certain price. Age and income are considered along with other factors when the FHA decides whether he will be able to repay the mortgage.

The application for the loan is made to any FHA-approved lender—not to FHA itself. If the lender is willing to make the loan, he provides the proper forms and helps the borrower fill them out. Then he forwards the papers to the FHA insuring office, which reviews the applicant's credit history and appraises the property to determine the amount of the mortgage which FHA will insure. The FHA then tells the lender what it has decided, and the lender informs the borrower. If FHA has approved the application, the lender arranges with the borrower for the closing of the loan. The borrower deals directly with the lender. The lender handles the transaction with FHA.

In January 1970, the maximum allowable interest rate

An aerial view of Reston, Virginia, an experiment in a new form of community life intended to recreate the cohesion and gracefulness of an old European village and thereby recover values shattered by urban disorder.

on an FHA-insured home mortgage was increased to 8½ percent. In addition, the FHA collects a mortgage insurance premium of ½ of 1 percent, bringing the total interest charge to 9 percent. The maximum interest rates change from time to time, depending on the supply of and demand for mortgage money. But the interest rate does not change on an individual's home mortgage after it has been insured.

With an FHA-insured loan, the minimum down payment on new homes is 3 percent of the first $15,000 of value, 10 percent for the next $5,000, and 20 percent for the remainder up to the maximum loan of $33,000. Most FHA-insured loans have thirty-year terms, but they also may be for ten, fifteen, twenty, twenty-five and, in a few cases, thirty-five years.

Conventional loans

Conventional mortgage loans are two-party deals between the borrower and the lender. No government guarantees back up the lender. If the buyer defaults on the loan, the lender is stuck with the house. At the same time, however, the lender is free to charge whatever interest he can get (within, of course, state usary laws), can decide what construction standards are required, and can determine what qualifies a buyer. In brief, he has more flexibility to adapt to the ever-changing money and housing markets. Of the more than $265 billion in outstanding home mortgage loans in 1969, about two-thirds —$175 billion—were conventional loans. FHA-insured loans accounted for 20 percent of the total; VA-guaranteed loans for 13.5 percent. The dominant role played by conventional loans· is seen also in these statistics: In 1968, 81 percent of all housing starts were financed by conventional loans; 15 percent were FHA-insured loans and only 4 percent were VA-guaranteed loans.

By far the biggest holder of conventional loans are savings and loan associations. Other lenders making conventional loans include commercial banks, mutual savings banks and life insurance companies, as well as such diverse organizations as pension funds, nonprofit institutions, credit unions, and real estate companies.

As a general rule, savings and loan associations require a smaller down payment on a conventional loan than other lenders, but they are likely to charge a slightly higher interest rate. Of course, this varies from one part of the country to another, and also is subject to fluctuations in the money market. One lender may be willing to grant 75 percent financing, while another may go to 90 percent. One may set a 20-year mortgage term; another may set a 25-year term. This is why it is important to shop around for a loan. If you fail to get a loan on the first try, you might try again later. The mortgage money picture often changes rapidly, and a lender who turned you down a few weeks earlier may reverse himself when approached again.

As you shop around for a mortgage, there are other factors you should bear in mind:

• Points. In periods of tight money, it is not unusual for a lender to charge a placement fee, known as "points" in the parlance of the real estate business, when he makes a VA or FHA loan. And in times of extremely tight money, points also are charged on conventional loans. This is a one-time charge. Each point is 1 percent of the amount of the mortgage. For instance, with a $20,000 mortgage, a charge of $400 would equal 2 points. These points generally are paid by the seller. But, obviously, if the seller is going to have to pay a substantial sum in points to arrange the mortgage, he is apt to increase the price of the house to cover the added expense.

• Prepayment clause. Inclusion of such a clause in a mortgage allows you to pay off part or all of the principal earlier than the schedule calls for. VA mortgages allow you to prepay without penalty. FHA mortgages let you prepay up to 15 percent of the principal in any one year, again without penalty. Many conventional mortgages charge a stiff penalty if you prepay the principal. The reason, of course, is that the lender loses interest charges—since interest is charged only on the unpaid balance.

• Open-end clause. This clause permits you to refinance the loan without paying new financing charges. This can come in handy if you want to refinance so you can expand the house or send a child to college.

Should you assume a loan?

Many home buyers face this question. There are some advantages in assuming an existing mortgage on a home and some disadvantages. The chief advantage for the buyer is the lower interest rate that the mortgage usually carries. For instance, many outstanding loans carry 5 percent, 5½ percent, or 6 percent interest rates, compared with 8 percent to 9 percent interest rates in effect in 1970. You also cut down closing costs when you assume a mortgage, although you have to pay a small fee for recording the deed and modifying the contract. And you can assume a VA loan even if you are not a veteran.

Some mortgages, however, contain a clause preventing such take-overs by requiring full repayment of the mortgage in the event of sale. And other mortgages include a clause stating that the mortgage may be assumed—but only at the going interest rate at the time of the assumption, if that rate is higher than the one in the original mortgage. Thus, if the original mortgage carried a 5 percent interest rate, you might have to pay a higher rate, say 8 percent, if you assume the mortgage. The reason for such a clause is obvious: lenders are not eager to continue a 5 percent mortgage when the current interest rate is much higher.

There is another common catch in assuming a loan. A hypothetical case will illustrate:

Ten years ago, Mr. Jones bought a $25,000 house, paying $5,000 down and taking out a $20,000 mortgage. Since then, he has reduced the mortgage to $15,000. Now Mr. Jones wants to sell the house. His asking price is $30,000. He is willing to let the buyer assume the mortgage, but to do so the buyer must come up with $15,000 cash. The question is: How many buyers are willing or able to come up with that amount of cash?

Second mortgages

The second mortgage can be the instrument that permits a buyer to assume an attractive existing mortgage. Continuing the previous illustration, here is how it works:

Mr. Smith was interested in buying Mr. Jones' $30,000 house, but had only $10,000 of the $15,000 needed to assume the low-interest existing mortgage. So Mr. Jones agreed to grant Mr. Smith a $5,000 second mortgage. The $5,000 is to be repaid in five years, and is called a second mortgage because it is in addition to the original, or "first," mortgage.

Sometimes builders take a second mortgage to make up the difference between the down payment required and the amount of cash the buyer has to put up. Second mortgages also can be obtained from some lenders, such as banks.

Second mortgages are of two general types: the amortizing mortgage and the "balloon" mortgage. The amortizing second mortgage is set up like a regular mortgage, except that the repayment period usually is shorter. The balloon mortgage is somewhat different. This is how a typical one works:

Joe Henry got a $1,000 second mortgage to make the down payment on his house. It was the balloon type, and was to be repaid in five years. The monthly payments were only $10—about half of what they would be with a fully amortized loan—but at the end of five years the mortgage would be only about one-third paid off. At that time, he would have to come up with the cash to pay off the remaining "balloon" portion of the loan. This, of course, could create some problems. But the balloon second mortgage sometimes is the answer in a situation where the buyer could not afford the property if he had to make the higher monthly payments on a fully amortizing five-year second mortgage.

Closing costs

When you have arranged financing on the house you plan to buy, you are ready for the final step—"closing," or, as it is sometimes called, "settlement." This is where the buyer and seller exchange documents and payments, and ownership passes from one to the other. There are "closing costs" involved in wrapping up the deal. This catch-all term covers the half-dozen or more items that have to be paid—in cash—when you take title to the property.

If you are making your first venture into homeownership, these closing costs can come as a jolt. In the Washington, D.C., area, you could pay about $1,200 in closing costs on a $37,000 house with a $30,000 mortgage. In the New York suburbs, real estate men say closing expenses on a $40,000 house run anywhere from $1,500 to $2,000. In Chicago, one big savings and loan association says closing costs on a $30,000 house run about $650. In other areas of the country, closing costs can be as low as $300. Several big builders now include closing costs in the purchase price if you buy a home in one of their developments.

Here are some of the items included in closing costs:

Mortgage processing charge: This fee may be called a mortgage service fee, initial service fee, brokerage fee, origination fee, or be known by some other designation. It reimburses the lender for the paperwork, time, and expense involved in handling your mortgage. It generally runs about 1 percent of the mortgage, but in some areas is higher.

Title insurance: Most lenders require you to buy what is known as mortgage title insurance. This protects the lender in case someone, at some time in the future, disputes ownership of the property. The policy covers the full amount of the mortgage principal. When the mortgage is paid off, the policy terminates.

Remember that mortgage title insurance protects the lender, even though the home buyer pays the policy premium. There is another type of policy which gives you, the owner, similar protection. It is called owner's title insurance, and it gives you lifetime protection against ownership disputes.

When you pay the title insurance premium, the company issues a policy assuring that it has searched every recorded instruction affecting title to your property—tax records, court decrees, wills, mortgages, transfers, and the like. If the title search failed to disclose some flaw in the title and there later is a lawsuit, the company will fight the suit for you. If the other party wins, the title company will pay.

Title insurance premiums vary. In one midwestern city, you can get a mortgage title policy on a moderate priced home for about $70.00. Then, for an extra $35.00 you can obtain an owner's policy. In one eastern state, a mortgage title policy costs $62.50 on a $25,000 mortgage. A combination policy, protecting both lender and owner, costs $112.00. Nationwide, the most frequently quoted rate for title insurance is $3.50 per $1,000 of the sale price.

Taxes and insurance: With an FHA or VA loan, escrow payments are required for property taxes and fire and hazard insurance. The maximum prepayment in any event would be for one year. If you buy the house midway through the tax year, the prepaid taxes would be half as much. On a conventional loan, the lender may not ask for escrow payments—although many now require them.

Lawyer's fees: If you hire a lawyer, his fee sometimes is included in the closing costs. Charges vary, but if you have received legal advice throughout negotiations you may pay from $50 to $200.

Survey fee: In some cases, the lender may require a survey made to determine lot lines, dimensions, and location of the house on the lot. The idea is to make certain they fit the description on the deed. For a typical lot, the survey may cost around $50. If the property has been surveyed before, the fee will be less.

Appraisal fee: The charge for the appraisal ordered by the lender when you were negotiating the loan is passed on to you at the time of closing. On an FHA or VA loan an appraisal is mandatory, and virtually all lenders want an appraisal on a conventional loan, too. The appraisal fee generally is from $20 to $50, but may be higher or lower depending on local practice.

Credit report: One of the first things a lender does when you apply for a mortgage is to check your credit rating. This usually is done through a local credit bureau, if you are a local resident, for a fee of anywhere from $5 to $15. If you are a new resident and your credit references are in a distant city, the fee may be several times that much.

When you have paid all of the closing costs, and signed all of the documents, the house is yours. You are handed the keys, and you can move in.

Tips on Selling

When the time comes to sell your house, should you try to sell it yourself, or should you turn immediately to a real estate agent?

Experts say you might consider trying to sell the house yourself if you are not in a hurry and can answer yes to most of these questions:

—Are houses in your area in demand?

—Is mortgage money generally obtainable?

—Is your house appealing and standard in its offerings?

—Do you have a particularly attractive feature, such as a big family room or a modernized kitchen?

—Is it springtime or early fall—the most likely time for buyers?

—Is the local school district good?

—Is your house located where a "For Sale" sign can be seen by Sunday drivers?

—Has selling by owner been successful in your area?

If you decide to try to sell the house yourself, it is best if you set a time limit—such as two to four weeks. After this time, you probably will have exhausted the local supply of potential buyers, as well as your enthusiasm.

It might be better to turn to a real estate agent from the start when:

—You must sell in a hurry.

—There are a lot of houses for sale in your area.

—Mortgage money is hard to arrange.

—It is mid-winter and fewer people are house-hunting.

—Your house is on an out-of-the-way street, or in a rural area.

—Your house lacks an important feature, such as a garage or extra bathroom.

Of course, the big advantage of selling the house yourself is that you save the percentage of the price that otherwise would go to a real estate agent as his commission. Generally speaking, the agent's commission will be about 6 percent of the selling price. However, the percentage varies in different parts of the country. For this fee, the broker handles many of the details involved in selling a house. He writes, places and pays for newspaper advertisements. He shows prospects through the house. He helps a prospective buyer obtain a mortgage. And because he has a list of house-hunters, he may be able to sell the house faster than you could on your own.

How do you find the right real estate agent?

There are an estimated 800,000 real estate agents in the United States—men and women, full-time and part-time, experienced and inexperienced. Selecting a good real estate agent can be difficult. These points may help in your search:

• Ask friends and neighbors who have bought or sold real estate to make recommendations. If they were pleased with the agent they dealt with, this is a good start.

• Ask several banks in the community if they can suggest a good real estate agent. Chances are that two or three names will be mentioned repeatedly.

• Look for an agency which has a well-located and well-maintained office, and look for evidence of dignified advertising and numerous "For Sale" signs.

One note here: The term "realtor" is commonly used to refer to any real estate agent, although it is a trademark designation indicating any individual or firm belonging to a local real estate board and to the National Association of Real Estate Boards (NAREB). Realtors subscribe to standards set by a group of local realtors. These standards are based on the realtors' national code of ethics.

Listings: open, exclusive, or multiple?

If you decide to use a real estate agent, you face still another question: which type of listing should be used?

Listings may be divided into three broad categories—open, exclusive, and multiple.

In the open type, you offer the listing to any number of agents. In essence, you promise to pay them the agreed commission if they produce a family ready, willing, and able to buy at the listed terms prior to the time the listing is cancelled or the house is sold. You should bear in mind, however, that agents are less likely to devote substantial time or money in promoting such a listing, since their chances of earning the commission are usually too uncertain. Conflicts also can develop over who is entitled to a commission on such a listing.

The exclusive listing may be of two types—an "exclusive agency" or an "exclusive right to sell." Under an exclusive agency listing, you agree that the agent you select shall be the only one with whom the house will be listed for a specified period of time. You do not, however, rule out the possibility of producing a buyer yourself· during this period. In the latter event, the agent is not entitled to a commission. To avoid disputes, you should be sure that the listing agreement clearly sets forth that you have such a right of sale. Under the exclusive right to sell listing, the agent is entitled to the commission on the sale of the property even if you find your own buyer through no effort of his.

The multiple listing has come into widespread use in recent years. It is a variation of the exclusive right to sell listing. With a multiple listing, you give an exclusive right to sell to an agent of your choice—known as the listing agent—for a specified period. Then, through the multiple listing agency, the listing is printed, sometimes together with a picture of the house, and is distributed to all agents in the community who are members of the multiple listing service. This means that although you have listed your property with only a single agent, it is placed in the hands of a great many agents. After the listing is distributed, all agents which belong to the service (it usually operates as an adjunct of the local Board of

Realtors) will have a chance to sell the property at the stated terms. This gives the property much broader exposure. The agent who produces the buyer—known as the selling agent—will then split the commission with the listing agent according to percentages set by the multiple listing service. If the listing agent also is the selling agent, he gets the full commission. This means he likely will be the agent who devotes the greatest effort to selling the house. For example, he is most likely to spend money advertising the house in a newspaper. Thus, even though you get wide exposure through the multiple listing service, you should select the best possible listing agent.

When you use the multiple listing service, you must agree to abide by certain regulations. For instance, you may be required to agree that the listing be in effect for at least 30, 60, or 90 days—even up to six months in some parts of the country. A minimum period like this is required for the service to have the listings printed and distributed and to permit a reasonable time for agents to line up prospects. If the seller wants to withdraw from the multiple listing before the minimum period expires, he usually must obtain the written consent of the listing agent. Multiple listing agreements normally provide that, even after the listing expires or is withdrawn, a liability for payment of a commission may arise if a person who inspected the property while it was listed decides to buy it within 120 days (or other specified period) after such termination. Such a requirement is essential to the successful operation of a multiple listing service and, experts say, should not be objected to by an honest seller. But before you sign a multiple listing agreement, you should make certain there are no unreasonable terms in any withdrawal provision. You can do this by asking the agent with whom you intend to list your property to give you a letter stating the conditions under which the listing may be withdrawn. If any of the stated conditions seem unreasonable, check the matter with your attorney before you give the listing.

What price should you set?

It is vitally important that you set a realistic price on

your home. In most cases, the price will determine how fast you will make the sale. You are operating at a marked disadvantage if you ask, say $30,000, for a house that may command only $25,000. If you retain a broker, he will help you set the price. If you are selling yourself, you need to take extra care in setting the price. Remember, you will be competing not only with other homeowners who are trying to sell their property themselves but also with professional agents who have much more experience and many more clients that you are apt to have.

You probably have some idea of what you think your house is worth. But this is not necessarily the price you should ask. Chances are you will tend to over-value your property. You will think of all the improvements you have put into it, and will expect to get your money back. And while improvements may add to the value, the major determining factor in setting the price is the competition. What are other similar houses selling for in your city? One way to find out is to visit other houses like yours which are for sale. It is best to do this when they are open for inspection, such as on weekends. Note the asking price and then later check courthouse records to see what the property sold for.

There are several factors to keep in mind, though, in making comparisons. For example, the other lot may be smaller or larger than yours; the other house may or may not have a garage; it may or may not have a fireplace; it may have a new furnace; it may have a remodeled kitchen. Items such as these affect the sales price.

Another way to get a reading on what your home is worth is to obtain an independent appraisal. You may retain a professional appraiser anywhere from $25 to $100. The appraiser will make a thorough check of the house, and he will analyze such factors as the values of other properties in the neighborhood.

There is still another way to get the benefit of professional expertise—without paying a fee. This can be done by calling three, four, or five qualified real estate brokers in your area, explaining to them that you want to sell your house, and would like to know what price you should ask for it. The brokers will make every effort to convince you

HOW DEMAND FOR HOUSING WILL GROW

A Projection of Number of U.S. Households

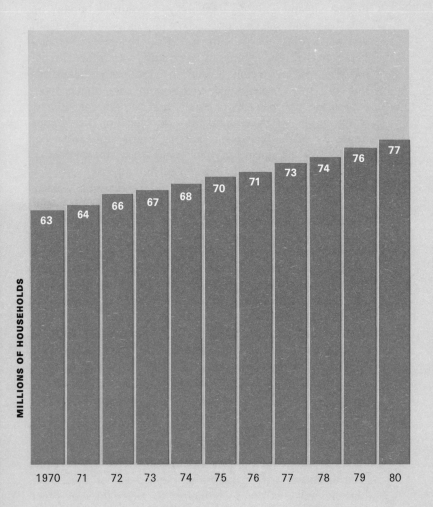

MILLIONS OF HOUSEHOLDS

| 1970 | 71 | 72 | 73 | 74 | 75 | 76 | 77 | 78 | 79 | 80 |
| 63 | 64 | 66 | 67 | 68 | 70 | 71 | 73 | 74 | 76 | 77 |

Source: U.S. Census Bureau

that you should list the house with them, but in any event probably will give you a figure they think the house is worth. Average out their prices and you will have some idea of what you should ask for your house. For example, suppose you contact three brokers. One tells you $20,000; another $20,500; and a third $19,500. Then the price you might consider is $20,000—the average of the three.

When you set a price, keep this point in mind: Many buyers do not expect to pay the first price quoted. They figure that the asking price will not be the final price, so you might add a little to your price to leave room for bargaining. But you are advised by experts not to overdo it. If you set the price too high, the buyer may lose interest and not even make a counter offer.

Aids for selling

The first step—whether you plan to try to sell the house yourself or list it with a real estate agent—is to prepare the house carefully for inspection by prospective buyers.

Experts stress this point: First impressions are important; they have a lasting effect on the would-be buyer.

The first impression often is based on the outside appearance of your house. You simply cannot rely on the buyer falling in love with the interior of the house. He may never stop to look unless he finds the exterior pleasing. So, experts say, it is important to ask yourself these questions:

—Is the exterior in need of a coat of paint?

—Are there loose hinges, shutters, or screens?

—Is the lawn neat?

—What about the shrubbery? Does it need trimming?

—Is the garage free of old tools, equipment, or odds and ends no longer used?

—Are the sidewalks free of debris or hazards like children's toys, ice, or snow?

A prospective buyer will not be in a receptive mood after he has tangled with an errant skate or with an icy spot. Besides, he could sue if he is injured in such an accident.

The interior appearance comes next in importance A clean, well-kept interior indicates a house has been properly maintained. The buyer could be so impressed with the tidiness that he may overlook some minor problems. Meticulous house cleaning takes more than a quick spin with the vacuum cleaner or a few swipes with the dust cloth. Special attention should be paid to the kitchen. A bright and tidy kitchen has special appeal to the ladies. Even middle-aged appliances look younger if they are sparkling clean.

Throughout the house, clean and shiny windows brighten up the interior. If it is necessary to repaint the interior, try to choose light, neutral colors. The buyer may turn around and immediately repaint with different colors, but clean, bright walls and woodwork are definite sales aids. Besides improving the appearance of the house, there is another important reason for repainting: If redecorating has to be done after the sale, the prospective buyer will be mentally deducting the cost from your asking price. And he will be calculating the cost on the basis of what a professional painter would charge. This will be several times the cost if you did the job yourself.

Today's modern, easy-to-apply paints do a remarkable job of covering small cracks in walls and ceilings. But it may be necessary to use other fillers to take care of more serious problems. Filling all cracks is important because prospective buyers view them as a sign of structural weakness—regardless whether this is the case.

Along with conspicuous cracks in walls, water spots on the ceiling are another factor damaging to sales appeal. In the buyer's mind, the spots mean the roof has leaked in the past—or still leaks. Telling him the roof has been repaired will do nothing to erase that first impression. So it is worth the expense to repaint the ceiling and remove the evidence of former problems. The same applies to damp spots in the basement. The prospect comes looking for these damp spots, and if he finds them he immediately envisions a flooded basement come the first rain storm. So, again, it pays to eliminate the cause of the dampness and repaint where needed.

In the basement you might also make certain that no cobwebs are lurking in the vicinity of the furnace or hot-water heater. A prospective buyer, spotting such an ac-

DEMAND OUTSTRIPS SUPPLY OF HOUSES

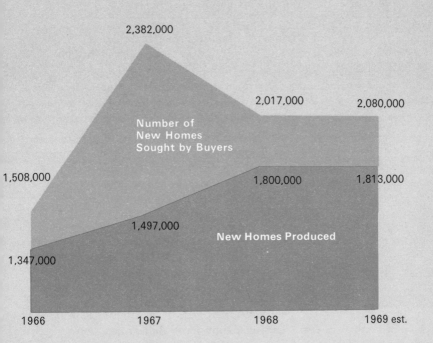

2,382,000

2,017,000   2,080,000

Number of
New Homes
Sought by Buyers

1,508,000

1,800,000   1,813,000

1,497,000

New Homes Produced

1,347,000

1966   1967   1968   1969 est.

In each of the last four years, production of new housing—apartments and mobile homes included—has fallen short of meeting demand. For the entire period, production has run an estimated 1.5 million behind demand.
In recent months, housing starts have begun to decline rapidly. Rents for apartments and prices of old and new houses are rising.

Note: Demand is based on number of units estimated for new households, "second homes," and replacement of homes that are demolished. Production includes net increase in mobile homes in use.

Source: National Association of Home Builders

cumulation of cobwebs, will wonder just how much time and trouble you have put into keeping up the house. After you clean out the cobwebs, you might neatly store or cart away the junk that is certain to have piled up in the basement.

Experts suggest these additional tips:

• Display the full value of your storage areas by making certain that closets are free of clutter. Overcrowded closets may give the unfair impression that there is not enough closet space.

• If you plan to show the house during the evening, it is wise to brighten it up with proper illumination—from the front porch light right on through the rest of the house.

• Loose knobs, leaking faucets, warped doors and windows give the impression of shoddy maintenance. Take a few minutes and repair these deficiencies.

• If you have an attractive fireplace and are showing your house in the cool months, try to keep a crackling fire going. This lends a coziness which adds to your home's appeal. But if you are selling in the warmer months, keep ashes and soot cleaned out of the fireplace. And polish up any brass fixtures.

• An attractive mirror, properly placed, can make your room look larger and can reflect and magnify many of your best selling points.

• Add the little touches that give a house that "homey" feeling. Examples are a vase of flowers, a plant, or small pillows. Don't go overboard and make the rooms look cluttered. Aim for a restful, happy look. Remember, don't just sell a house—sell a home.

• Think back to the qualities you looked for when you bought your house. These will be the same your prospective buyers will be seeking—namely, a neat home in reasonably good condition that can be occupied without doing too much to it.

Another factor to be considered when you think about fixing up your house: expenses incurred for the specific purpose of selling your house can be deducted when it comes time to report, for income tax purposes, how much profit you made on the sale.

Advertising your house for sale

The most frequently used method of advertising houses for sale is in the classified section of local newspapers. If you look through the classified pages, you will see that ads placed by successful real estate agents follow the same pattern. Their ads are designed to get the reader's attention, arouse his interest, and stimulate action by him. If you try to sell your own house, you should try to do the same in your ads. Remember, too, to ask yourself, "What type of person is most likely to be attracted to this house?" Then aim your ad at that type person.

Real estate advertising experts have come up with this set of guidelines to follow in preparing your ad:

1. Be honest. Careful choice of words can add spice to the ad, but make certain that they do not make it less factual.

2. Make yourself clearly understood. Provide all pertinent information the reader needs. For example, say "six blocks north of expressway," rather than "exclusive north section." This may take a few more words, but it should pay off in more responses to your ad.

3. Get right to the point. Most people are too busy to plow through wordy essays. Also, try to make the ad interesting. Papers carry so many ads that people skip the dull ones.

4. Be enthusiastic, but don't try to be funny or cute. Tell the reader what he wants to know in a pleasant way.

5. Keep sentences short. Twelve words should be about the maximum. This keeps your ad from sounding too complicated.

6. After you have written your ad, pause and read it to yourself. Then ask yourself whether it provides factual, honest information in simple, concise language. If it does, you may have a good ad.

Should you list your price in the ad?

Experts generally say yes. They point out that including the price in the ad will help limit the flow of lookers to the serious prospects. For instance, a family which plans to buy a $30,000 house will not want to spend time looking at a $15,000 home. And, conversely, families interested in buying a $15,000 house will refrain from inspecting one costing twice that much.

What other specifics should be included in the ad?

Perhaps the most important is the approximate location of the property. Next is the number of bedrooms, then the type of house—two-story, ranch style, Cape Cod, etc.—and whether it has a basement, garage, or family room; and the type of heat—gas, oil, or electric.

Obviously, you want to get responses only from those prospects who are interested in your type of home, in your type of neighborhood, and in your price range. So your ad should be specific enough to let the market know what you are offering.

Here are examples of a good ad and a poor ad:

GOOD
By Owner

Sunset Heights, four bedrooms. Cape Cod, gas heat, full basement, 2-car garage, large kitchen w/eating space, family room w/fireplace, large yard. $24,000. Call 938-7684.

POOR
Dream House

Immaculately beautiful dream home in the city's most exclusive residential neighborhood. This one has everything you want and is a bargain that you won't want to miss, so call 938-7684 today.

You can readily see that the good ad is brief and to the point, providing information that most buyers want—location, number of bedrooms, type of house, type of heating, and whether there is a basement. The poor ad is approximately the same length, yet it contains none of the specifics listed in the good ad.

Another effective advertising medium can be the "For Sale" sign in front of your house. If you are selling your house yourself, a professionally made sign is a wise investment. The sign should be large enough to be read from a passing car. It should be in bright colors to catch the eye. It should list your telephone number, and it should contain the words "By Owner." It would seem logical that, if a broker's name is not on the sign, the passerby would assume the owner is selling the house himself. Yet the words "For Sale By Owner" provide added insurance that the message gets across.

There is still another way to advertise your home—by word of mouth. This costs nothing, yet it can be a most effective way of selling your home. It does, however, require effort. Here are some tips on how to conduct a word-of-mouth advertising campaign:

• Tell all of your friends and neighbors that you are selling your house. They probably have noticed the "For Sale" sign in the yard, but a brief chat may enlist them as active allies in your cause. They might have house-hunting friends in another part of town they would like to have as neighbors.

• Tell your mailman, milkman, minister, barber or hair dresser, newspaper delivery boy. They come in contact with many other families, some of whom may be in the market for a house.

• Post notices on bulletin boards at your place of employment, your church, and your neighborhood supermarket. Besides giving specific information on the house, you might attach a snapshot of the property.

Tips on showing the house

Before you start showing your house, you may want to prepare a detailed fact sheet to give to prospective buyers. The fact sheet could include:

—Basic financial information, such as the amount of the mortgage and monthly payments and the interest rate, if you are willing to let the buyer assume the loan.

—The assessed valuation of the property, and the tax rate.

—The "extras" which go with the house. Examples might be drapes, carpets, and appliances.

—The average cost of electricity, heat and water; and the age of the furnace and hot water heater.

—The location of nearby schools, churches, shopping centers, parks, and other recreational areas.

In addition to this fact sheet, you may want to prepare a sketch of the floor plan, including the number and size of closets, the location and size of windows and doors, and the dimensions of each room. Be as clear and accurate as you can in preparing the sketch. For a few cents a sheet, you can have additional copies made of the fact sheet and floor plan sketch. You would then have a supply on hand to distribute to prospective buyers who look at the house. The sheets would answer the most-often-asked questions.

How frequently you show your home, and when, is up to you. You can specify in your advertisements when the home is open for inspection such as from 2 to 6 p.m. on Sunday, or you can accept appointments any time that is mutually convenient.

When showing your home, answer honestly all questions raised by prospective buyers. Never misstate the condition of your house or the neighborhood. Frank, honest answers instill confidence; dishonest or misleading answers destroy it. And, successful salesmen say, generating confidence is a key to making the sale.

Let the prospect take his time in examining the house. If he overlooks an important feature, tell him about it. You need not volunteer unnecessary information. You can be a friendly guide without torrents of comment and chatter. The old saying, "silence is golden," applies here.

Above all, listen. By listening to what the prospect says, you can get a good idea of what he wants in a house. Then you can stress those points and the job of selling will be easier.

You can also adopt some of the techniques of master salesmen. This is one: Ask a question that can be answered with an affirmative response. Avoid questions which will bring a negative response.

For instance, pose questions like these:

"Isn't this a bright, sunny kitchen?"

"This is certainly a large workshop, isn't it?"

Everytime you solicit a yes answer from the prospect, you have taken another step toward making a sale. And you will be taking giant strides if you are able to condition the prospect's mind to action by having him say and do things that point to action. This is what psychologists call activation, and every successful salesman, in any field, employs it without fail.

For example, have the prospect do things, look at things, feel things, measure things. Have him stroll across the lawn. Have him look through the picture window. Have him open the furnace door. Have him feel the thick pile of the carpet. Everytime he does something for himself, he is selling himself.

How trade-ins work

If you are selling one house and buying another, you may run into a difficult problem in timing. You do not want to move out of your old house until you can move into the new one. And you do not want to buy a new one until you have sold the old one.

One solution is to use the trade-in method. Anyone who has ever traded in an older automobile for a new one is familiar with the general principle of the deal. But house trade-ins are more complex than car trade-ins, so you may find it necessary to retain a real estate agent.

Here is how a typical trade-in might work:

Al Spencer and his wife decided their present home was too small for their growing family. So they went house-hunting, and found a new and larger house they liked. But the Spencers realized they would be unable to sign a commitment to buy the new house until they knew that their old house had been sold on terms which would permit them to make the new purchase. Selling the old home first, then buying the new one, seemed an unsatisfactory approach. The new house may no longer be available by the time the sale of the old one is completed. Their inability to plan the change in occupancy created problems. Nevertheless, they worked out this solution:

The Spencers sign a contract to buy the new house subject to receiving a satisfactory trade-in agreement on the old house. The broker handling the sale of the new house makes an appraisal of the Spencers' smaller home. He then issues a commitment to buy the property at a "guaranteed price" on or before a date which meets the Spencers' requirements for the new home. Prior to the deadline, the broker attempts to sell the property at a higher "recommended price." This will be something close to the appraised market value. The agreement states that even if the broker does not make the sale by deadline, he will pay the Spencers the "guaranteed price," which is lower than the "recommended price" to permit the broker a margin of safety if he is required to purchase the home.

The terms of any trade agreement, of course, can be varied to fit the particular needs of the trading owner. But, in general, the less the agreement requires of the broker in the way of guarantee, the higher the broker can make the ultimate price. For instance, it is not uncommon for trade agreements to require the broker to put up only enough money to cover the down payment and closing costs on the new home. The agreement then provides that the owner will receive the balance of his equity from the old home when it is sold by the broker or, if not sold, then at the end of a specified period, such as one or two years.

Trade-ins usually involve two properties within the same city. But, in this age of mobility, it is not uncommon for them to involve homes in two different cities. These inter-city trades make use of essentially the same type of agreement, except that it involves cooperating brokers in two cities. The brokers work out an arrangement between themselves for splitting commissions and profits on the old home being sold and on the new one being purchased. This way brokers are able to offer the homeowner a high enough "guaranteed price" for the old home to make such a trade practical.

Besides two homes, either in the same or different cities, trades can involve other kinds of property such as vacant lots, mobile homes, or automobiles. Real estate agents report that such trades are worked out with some frequency and, depending on individual circumstances, merit serious consideration.

**Vacation Homes
for Fun
and Investment**

Millions of Americans own not one house, but two.

According to Census Bureau figures, an estimated 1.7 million families have second homes. And the number is steadily growing as other families acquire second homes at a rate of more than 150,000 a year.

These second homes come in all types and sizes. They range from primitive hunting cabins to modern A-frame ski lodges to lakeside cottages to expensive glass-fronted beach houses. Their costs go from a few hundred dollars to hundreds of thousands of dollars.

There are sound reasons for this trend. In the first place, a piece of real estate is usually a good investment. This is especially true if it is located in a popular recreational area. Second, and perhaps most important, is the desire of city dwellers to "get away from it all" by heading for the great outdoors.

Stewart Udall, when he was secretary of the interior, summed it up this way:

> Only a few years ago, when our population was predominately rural, our recreation needs were different. All we had to do to shoot quail was to grab the old double-barrel out of the closet and go down

through the field until we flushed a covey.

But now we are urbanized and our total numbers have increased amazingly. We live in cities or in what we sometimes call "slurbs." We have more spendable money than we used to. We work shorter hours, have more leisure time on our hands. And we have mobility. Our car can transport us over super-highways which give us a one-day range hardly to be imagined a bare generation ago.

We possess an ingrown, almost mystic yearning to get into the out-of-doors. It is our heritage. The out-of-doors offers perhaps the most desirable outlet which could be devised for effective, constructive use of the increased leisure time which is now ours.

Census Bureau surveys have turned up some interesting statistics on the rush of American families to fulfill the yearning for a second home. A nationwide study a few years ago showed that:

—Most second homes are described by their owners as either a "house" or a "vacation cottage." Houses comprise 33 percent of all second homes and cottages account for 57 percent. The remainder are described as "other" types, such as cabins or ski lodges.

—Eight out of ten second homes are single-story structures. The average value of second homes is $7,800. Three out of ten are valued at less than $5,000; and one out of ten at $20,000 or more.

—Nine out of ten have electricity but only six out of ten are equipped with running water and inside bath. About eight out of ten have some type heating equipment, but only two out of ten have a central heating system.

—Two out of three are located in the same state as the owners' primary residence. About 30 percent are within 50 miles of the first home. Nearly 60 percent are within 100 miles, and about 80 percent are within 200 miles.

—Seven out of ten families use their second homes in the summer only. About 25 percent use the second home in several seasons. About half the second homes were used 30 to 90 days a year. About one-fourth were used for less than 30 days, and only a few were used for more

DISTRIBUTION OF 1.55 MILLION SECOND HOMES IN U.S.

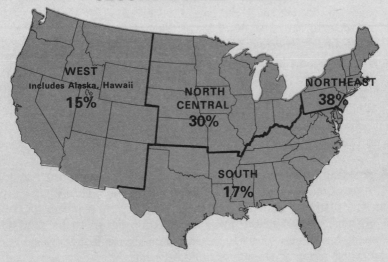

WEST
Includes Alaska, Hawaii
15%

NORTH CENTRAL
30%

NORTHEAST
38%

SOUTH
17%

DETAILS ABOUT SECOND HOMES
(By Regional Location)

Characteristic	Northeast	North Central	South	West
Owned second homes, total in thousands	542	474	245	235
Percent				
With electricity	88%	93%	95%	85%
With running water, toilet, and bathtub or shower	57	47	77	63
With central heating	24	19	25	14
With no heating equipment	19	11	15	11
1-story building	73	87	67	86
Built 1960 or later	20	25	39	28
Held for seasonal use only	71	72	44	47
Held for occasional use year round	22	20	46	42
Median				
Number of rooms	4.3	3.7	4.4	3.4
Value	$7,800	$7,000	$9,700	$7,400

Source: U.S. Department of Commerce, Bureau of the Census

U.S. Department of Agriculture, Forest Service

than 180 days.

—More than 90 percent of the heads of families owning second homes are over thirty-five years of age. More than 20 percent are sixty-five years of age and over.

—As can be expected, families with second homes have higher incomes than those without second homes. The average income of those with second homes is $9,600, compared with $5,900 for other families.

While the main reason most families buy a second home may be to "get away from it all," there are other factors. One is the investment aspect of such a purchase.

A vacation home as an investment

A vacation home can be a solid investment. This is especially true if you buy property located in a popular recreation area. Here the price appreciation is apt to be even more than the 5 to 10 percent annual rise that you can expect of many parcels of prime real estate.

Many families use their vacation homes only one, two, or three months a year. The rest of the time, they rent out the property. This can be rewarding from a financial standpoint. It is not unusual for a two-bedroom bungalow to bring $200 or more a week in Florida in season. The same prices prevail for many other ocean-front properties. In fact, real estate agents on the south shore of Long Island say a summer house there goes for $2,000 a season. And the property need not be on the beach. A ski chalet in a mountain resort area, for example, also could rent for $200 a week in the winter.

From an investment standpoint, the best vacation properties are to be found in the sunshine states—California, Florida, and Arizona. You can rent out these properties all year. Yet even where the vacation season is shorter, as in northern states, rental vacation homes are in demand.

Top rental property, of course, will be located near beaches, lakes, rivers, or ski areas. Besides location, however, it is important that the property be well-maintained. Families looking for a cottage to rent will shun run-down property. Therefore, upkeep will pay off. Generally, the entire vacation home will be rented to a family. But in some cases, individual bedrooms are rented out separately.

The Sea Ranch, a condominium of vacation homes on the northern Sonoma Coast, north of San Francisco, California.

To do this, though, each bedroom should have its own bathroom and private entrance. Either way, you will be expected, as the owner, to furnish linens, towels, and cooking utensils. One note here: If you have valuable furnishings in the vacation house, it is best to place them in a locked storage area when the home is being rented.

To rent out the property, you may want to retain a local real estate agent. For his commission—anywhere from 6 to 15 percent of the rental income, depending on the locality—he will take care of all the details. You can, of course, handle rentals yourself. But it will take time. In some instances, you will need to advertise in newspapers or local magazines. Often, though, word-of-mouth advertising is sufficient.

You can claim substantial tax deductions on property you rent out. These tax breaks apply to vacation homes which are rental property. Perhaps the biggest deductions are obtained by applying depreciation allowances to your vacation home and furnishings. Generally, depreciation on the house is spread over forty years. Depreciation on the furnishings is spread over ten years. The percentage of the depreciation you can take depends on how much your family uses the vacation home. Here is an example:

Joe Smith has a vacation home which his family uses three months—or 25 percent—of the year. The rest of the year he rents the house, so he can charge off 75 percent of the depreciation. The house cost $10,000, not counting the land, and the furnishings were worth $3,000, so he figures his depreciation deduction this way—

First he calculates 75 percent of $10,000 (the value of the house), or $7,500, and then he divides this by forty years, the number of years depreciation is allowed. This gives him $187.50 he can deduct each year as depreciation on the house.

Then he calculates 75 percent of $3,000 (the value of the furnishings), or $2,250, and divides by 10, the number of years depreciation is allowed on furnishings. This gives him $225, which he adds to the $187.50 deduction for depreciation of the house. Thus, his total deduction for depreciation is $412.50.

In addition, Mr. Smith can deduct 75 percent of the cost

of taxes, interest, insurance, utilities, maintenance, and cleaning of the property. And he can deduct the full cost of any real estate fees or advertising expenses he paid to rent out the property. Now, if the rental income he realizes is greater than these deductions, he must pay income taxes on any profit. But if the deductions are larger than the rental income, he can report a loss on the rental operation. This loss can be offset against his regular income, and thus help reduce his tax bill.

This example shows how depreciation and deductions work. And it illustrates how your vacation home can be a handsome investment from a tax standpoint.

A home on a golf course?

Some families are finding a pleasant mix between the attributes of a vacation home and a city home. They are building homes adjacent to golf courses.

Homesites along the fairways are enjoying increasing popularity—so much so that many builders are planning golf courses as part of their housing developments, even though a championship golf course may cost as much as $1 million to create.

For the golfing enthusiast, there is the obvious advantage of having a course in his own back yard. But there are other advantages for golfers and non-golfers alike.

Generally, such a location provides a sizeable, beautifully landscaped area around the home, often an attractive view, all without need of maintenance. The fairways also provide a buffer against commercial development. And there may be a heightened sense of privacy because the homesite adjoins the course itself, rather than a neighbor's backyard.

There are some drawbacks. A golf course attracts golfers. On weekends or sunny summer days, the golf course might generate considerable traffic in the neighborhood. And not all golfers drive straight down the fairway. Some slice, some hook, and golf balls just could land in your living room. Before signing up for a piece of golf course property, it would be a good idea to check the location carefully for possible nuisance or hazard, and to determine whether screening or fencing will be allowed if desired for safety and privacy.

Marketing men say home buyers are especially receptive to the homesite golf course.

At one recreational development halfway between Washington, D.C., and Richmond, Virginia, an eighteen-hole golf course was created as part of the initial development. The developers reported that there were not enough lots around the golf course to satisfy the demand. Buyers seemed to prefer the golf course sites to lots on one of the four lakes in the development.

The same was true at a new development about an hour's drive from Chicago. The developers found that lots which overlook or are adjacent to the eighteen-hole golf course are more popular than lots adjoining one of the several lakes they built. As the marketing manager put it: "There's much to be said for having a vast backyard which is very quiet in the evening, beautifully maintained by someone else in the spring and summer, and a snow-blanketed haven for rabbits in the winter."

What do you want in a vacation home?

If you have decided that you are going to buy a vacation home—even if it means forgetting about that new car or new furniture—the next thing to do is to answer this question: What is it you really want?

Is it a cabin in the mountains?

A cottage by the lake?

A house on the beach?

A chalet near a skiing slope?

A hunting shack on a duck marsh?

There are advantages and disadvantages to each type of vacation home. Everyone has his individual preferences. But there are several factors to consider in making a decision.

Can you tolerate neighbors nearby, or do you want complete privacy? Put another way, do you want a place with many of the conveniences of the city, or do you want a place out of sight and sound of civilization—where the only sounds that disturb the silence are produced by a gurgling brook and a busy woodpecker?

Do you want a vacation home you can reach in an hour or so? Or do you mind driving all day to get there? Will you compromise by locating within a three-hour drive of home?

The amount of money you have to spend may limit your choices. For instance, if you want a beachfront home an hour's drive from the city, you can figure on its being expensive. But if you are satisfied with a small tract of wooded land some distance from the city, you might be surprised how low the cost is. If you find that money is a problem, you might be able to interest another family or two in a cooperative project. An example: Three midwestern families pooled their money and bought a lodge on a lake, property that was beyond the means of any one of them alone. Obviously, there are disadvantages in such a joint arrangement. But partial ownership of a vacation home may be better than nothing.

Often, the first step toward getting a vacation home is to purchase a piece of property—a lakefront or beachfront lot, for example, or a wooded hillside tract. But before you plunk down your hard-earned cash for a piece of land, you should be aware of possible pitfalls—and how to avoid them.

Checklist for the unwary buyer

The national Better Business Bureau has prepared a checklist for the unwary land buyer. It raises questions which the buyer should have answered before he buys land by mail or after personal inspection. The checklist covers these factors:

1. *The promoter:* Who is behind the offer and the promotion? What have the experience and performance records of these persons been? Know with whom you are dealing. If you don't know, consult the local Better Business Bureau, Chamber of Commerce, or real estate board in the area.

2. *Advertising:* If there are advertised or pictured improvements, such as paved roads, marinas, parks, beaches, golf courses, or club houses, have they been completed, and are they currently available for use? Or are they simply planned if the development is successful? Is there

assurance that planned advertised improvements will be completed? Is the status of improvements indicated clearly? Do pictures in advertising show actual portions of the development? Are distances from facilities noted accurately, or are they described as "nearby" or "at your doorstep?" If prices are featured in advertising, is one lot of sufficient area for a house? Are you required to buy more than one lot?

3. *Location:* Exactly where is the property located? Is access assured? How far from highway? From town? From factories and industrial areas? From an airport or other transportation facilities? From shopping centers or diversified neighborhood stores? From other lots and homes? From civic and community facilities such as schools, churches, hospitals, police and fire protection, recreational facilities, etc.? How far from employment? Is the map upon which the lot is designated a recorded plat? If so, where has it been filed? If beach rights and water privileges are included, are they included in the filed map, and does the promoter have the right to grant such rights and privileges? Is the property located in an area where you will be troubled by insect pests? Would it be undesirable because of floods? What are the future plans for the area?

4. *Value of land in the area:* What is the current selling price of unimproved land in the immediate area of your lot? Is the price of lots in which you are interested in line with the price of other available land in the immediate vicinity? Are homes in the area well maintained? Is the character of the neighborhood satisfactory? Are the surroundings desirable?

5. *Status of property:* Who owns the land? Is it free and clear? If mortgaged, insist on knowing the exact terms from the holder. Are there any easements, liens, judgments, assessments, unpaid taxes, etc.? The title should be searched before any transaction is completed. The work of examining titles is generally done by lawyers or title companies. The purchase of property without certification by a lawyer or the obtaining of title insurance involves many risks that should be avoided.

6. *Improvements:* What improvements have been in-

stalled to date? Paved streets? Sidewalks? Street lights? Public utilities? Sanitary sewers? Storm sewers? Are there water mains, or must individual wells be dug? How much will a well cost? Are the tax assessments and the utility rates satisfactory? If improvements have been installed, have they been paid for? If not, what portion of the burden are property owners expected to share? If they have not been installed, what plans have been made for such installation, and what arrangements concerning the cost have been made? Has a bond been filed with state or county authorities to insure completion of improvements? Who will be responsible for maintenance of improvements, utilities, etc.? Is this set forth in writing?

7. *Sewers:* Are there sanitary sewers or must septic tanks be put in? If septic tanks are necessary, are they authorized by local zoning statutes? Is the level of the land and type of soil suitable for septic tanks? Is local health department approval required for septic tanks? Has such approval been granted?

8. *Drainage:* Is the land dry or must it be drained? Is drainage feasible and possible? Have storm sewers been installed? Does the situation and location of the plot permit effective drainage after storms? Is the water table sufficiently deep so that basement and foundations are above it?

9. *Soil and topography:* What is the top soil analysis? Is it satisfactory for lawn and garden? What about the subsoil? Does the property contain fill? If so, is there likelihood of sinkage? What is the topography of the land? Will it need grading, excavating, or filling? Retaining walls? What will the cost be? Is there a rock problem?

10. *Taxes:* What is the present tax assessment rate? What is the assessed value of the property? Will the assessed value increase when the property is improved? When civic and community improvements have been completed? What increase may be expected? Have special assessments been levied? If included in the purchase price, have they been paid? Are others in prospect?

11. *Financing:* If you are asked to pay so much down and so much per month over a period of years, insist on knowing the full details of such an arrangement. If a

down payment is required, you may wish to discuss with your attorney the advisability of placing such payments in escrow. Are the terms of the contract subject to your ability to obtain a satisfactory mortgage from a lender of your choosing? Is there a prepayment clause? Are its provisions satisfactory? It is important that the purchaser know not only whether he can obtain a mortgage but also whether there is an existing mortgage on the property. If so, must the buyer assume the mortgage, or will the seller satisfy the mortgage and discharge its lien? What are the alternatives? How much are the closing costs? Can they be included in the mortgage? If there is no mortgage, what are the carrying charges, if any, on the unpaid balance, on a time-payment plan? Is it advisable to retain an attorney for arranging and closing the mortgage transaction?

12. *Zoning:* What are the local zoning restrictions, and what protection do they offer? Will you have to buy more than one lot in order to comply with such zoning requirements? Will you have to buy more land in order to build the house you want, and still conform to local zoning regulations regarding the amount of frontage and the sidelines of the property? Are there any restrictive or protective convenants? What are their terms? Does your contemplated construction violate them?

More tips on site selection

If you follow the above checklist, you will be able to avoid many of the pitfalls of buying land for a vacation home. Here is another tip from the experts: Be sure to buy a big enough piece of land. Unless you control enough land around your vacation home, you will not be assured the privacy you may want. Here is an example:

Twenty years ago, a family bought a 70-foot lot on a lake in the midwest. They thought that would be plenty of land, since there were no other homes—vacation or otherwise—for miles around. But over the years, many other families bought lakeside lots. Now this family is completely surrounded by a subdivision of vacation homes—in fact, they have less elbow room at the lake than they have at home in the city.

Of course, land costs may force you to compromise somewhat on your desire for privacy. But this is a point to keep in mind when looking for a vacation homesite.

You should make certain, too, that you have ready access to your land. It does little good to own a choice 40-acre tract if it can be reached only by passing through other people's property. Experts say that before you buy any land, you should make sure that you either have a right-of-way to the land or can establish one without too much expense. Remember, too, that a dirt trail that may be easy to negotiate in the dry summer months can become completely impassable when it rains or snows.

What about utilities? Are they available at the site, or must they be installed, perhaps at great expense? Some people long for a mountaintop or beachfront retreat—but shudder at the thought of roughing it without electricity. The day is coming, experts say, when you may have the remote hideaway complete with all the comforts of city living —hot water, heat, air conditioning, washer, dryer, or any other electrical device. This will be possible through an independent generating system now under development. One prototype power system is about the size of a large freezer chest. It burns natural gas or fuel oil, generating steam which can be converted into either hot air or hot water, and propel a steam turbine to generate electricity for appliances. The cost may be about $2,000 per unit.

Final Considerations

Planning and building a vacation home from scratch can be a pleasant experience. There is an infinite variety of designs to choose from. You can rough out your own floor plan, or you can buy blueprints from your lumber dealer or through the mail. The chief considerations will be your needs and the amount of money you can spend.

If your family is small and you have only limited funds to work with, you might want to start with a single room home, perhaps about 12 by 20 feet—about the size of a garage. The main problem here is that it is difficult to separate sleeping quarters from living quarters with a single room design. So you may want to begin with a two-room design. In either case, it is best to pick a design which will allow you to add other rooms later.

Remember to provide plenty of storage space. And bear in mind that your design should be indigenous to your region. For example, a design with an expanse of glass wall may be great for a southern beach home, but it could make the same house almost impossible to heat in the north. Or a flat-roofed design that is no problem in the south may cave in under the weight of snow in the north. And a steep-roofed ski chalet may be perfect for the mountainside, but look out of place among lakeshore cottages.

When you have settled upon a design and floor plan for your vacation home, you are ready to decide how to go about having it built. There are three general methods of construction. First is the conventional way—on-site assembly of raw materials. Second is to use pre-cut materials. Everything is cut to the right size before being transported to the home site, where it is assembled. The third method is to use pre-fabricated construction, where building components like walls and roof trusses are assembled in a plant and delivered to the building site.

What will the costs be? They will vary greatly, depending on the size and type of vacation home you are building, on the materials used, and on the price of labor in different areas. As one rule of thumb, you can figure that a vacation home, complete and ready to occupy, will cost from $15 to $20 per square foot. Some barebone designs will cost less, but it is best to have a safe margin for error.

You may also ask, "Should I build my vacation home myself, or should I have it done?" If you are a handyman and have plenty of time, then you probably will want to do much of the work yourself. Of course, you may call in professionals for such jobs as laying a concrete slab. But you can cut down on costs by doing some of the easy tasks yourself. You can even enlist other members of the family, making it a family project. It could be a prelude to many hours and days of enjoyment you and your family will find at your vacation home.

Glossary

ABSTRACT OF TITLE—A history of the recorded instruments, such as deeds, wills and lawsuits, affecting ownership of a piece of property.

ADVANCE COMMITMENT—An agreement by which the lender agrees to grant a mortgage loan, at a specified interest rate, to the home buyer. It becomes effective when the buyer takes title to the property.

AGREEMENT OF SALE—The word "agreement" is identical in meaning with the word "contract."

AMORTIZATION—Paying back a debt by installment payments. Most of today's mortgages are monthly amortizing, which means interest is paid monthly along with repayment of the principal.

APPRAISAL—A written statement of estimated value made by a trained and experienced person.

APPRAISER—An expert who, for a fee, estimates the value of property.

APPRECIATION—An increase in the value of property due to factors unrelated to the improvements on the land.

ASSESSED VALUE—The value set on property by local assessors, normally a fraction of the actual market value. The property tax imposed is a rate of the assessed value.

BINDER—An agreement by which the buyer and seller tentatively agree on the terms of a contract. In some states, if for some valid reason, the contract cannot be drawn, the agreement is no longer enforceable.

CARRYING CHARGES—Cost incidental to home ownership, as taxes, insurance, maintenance.

CHATTEL—Any property, tangible or otherwise, except real estate.

CLOSING—In real estate transactions, this is the time at which the buyer completes payment to the seller and the seller delivers the deed to the buyer.

CONDOMINIUM—A form of complete ownership by which the buyer has the entire undivided interest in an apartment or similar type of dwelling—as opposed to ownership of the land upon which the dwelling sits.

CONTRACT—An enforceable agreement between two or more competent persons by which each promises to do or not to do a particular thing.

CONVEYANCE—Transfer of ownership of real property.

COMMISSION—A sum or percentage allowed an agent for his services. In real estate, it is a payment to a broker for selling property.

COOPERATIVE—Also called "co-ops," an apartment house where the occupants participate in ownership and cost of occupancy in proportion to the rental value of the space they occupy.

COVENANT—Any promise or agreement, usually applied to specific promises within a deed.

DEED—A written instrument that transfers ownership of property. The two most common types of deeds are the quitclaim deed, which relinquishes or releases to another only the seller's present interest in the land; and the warranty deed, in which the seller warrants the title against all claims of all persons whatsoever.

DEED OF TRUST—See trust deed.

DEFAULT—Failure to perform an act or obligation legally required, such as to meet payments on a mortgage loan or to comply with provisions of a sales agreement.

DEPRECIATION—The loss in value of property resulting from age, physical decay, changing neighborhood conditions or other causes.

EASEMENT—A legal term denoting the use of land in a certain way by someone other than the land owner.

EMINENT DOMAIN—The power of a municipal, state or federal government to take property for public use by condemnation proceedings.

EQUITY—The value of property, less any outstanding mortgages, liens or other changes.

ESCROW—A system by which the buyer submits the purchase price to a disinterested third party who disburses it to the seller after the title has been correctly passed to the purchaser.

EXCLUSIVE LISTING—The right given to a broker by a property owner to sell the property to the exclusion of any and all other brokers.

FEE SIMPLE—Absolute ownership of land.

LEASE—An agreement by which the lessor (landlord) grants possession for a period of time to the lessee (tenant), in return for rental payments.

LEASEBACK—An arrangement under which the tenant agrees to pay an amount of yearly rent which is calculated to pay off the mortgage and leave the property free and clear in the owner's hands after a stipulated number of years.

LEVERAGED—A property is said to be highly leveraged when the owner's cash equity is small in relation to the total value of the property.

LIEN—A hold or claim against a property as security for some debt or charge.

LIQUIDITY—The state of having cash available for use.

MARKET VALUE—The price at which the property might be reasonably sold if offered for sale in a fair market.

MECHANIC'S LIEN—A lien or claim by a contractor, subcontractor of workman for labor done or materials furnished which must be paid by a builder before he can sell to a home buyer.

MORTGAGE—A lien on real property which an owner gives a lender as security for the repayment of the money which the owner borrowed from the lender. The buyer or owner is called the mortgagor; the lender is the mortgagee.

MULTIPLE LISTING—An agreement by which one of a group of agents has an exclusive right to sell for a specified period; however, any one of the group can sell the property, but he must share the commission with the exclusive broker.

NOTE—A written instrument in which the signer promises to pay a specified sum to a specific person on a specific date. Usually, a home owner has executed a note as a part of the mortgage loan.

OPEN LISTING—Permission granted a broker to offer property for sale on a non-exclusive basis.

PERCENTAGE LEASE—A lease under which the tenant is required to pay as rental a specified percentage of the gross income from total sales made on the premises.

PLAT—A map showing planned use of land.

POINT—A one-time charge of 1 percent of the amount loaned. It is paid by the seller.

REALTOR—A real estate broker who is licensed by the state.

TITLE—The evidence by which the owner proves his ownership as well as his right to possession.

TITLE CERTIFICATE—A written statement prepared by an attorney or title company stating who has ownership of property.

TITLE INSURANCE—Insurance written by a title company to compensate the lender or owner for any loss if the property is owned by a person other than the seller, subject to conditions of policy.

TRUST DEED—In some states, this is a substitute for a mortgage. The buyer deeds the property to a third party, usually a title or escrow company, who holds it as a guarantee to the lender that the buyer will repay what he borrowed.

USURY—Charging more than the lawful rate of interest.

VENDEE—One who buys property.

VENDOR—One who disposes of property by sale.

ZONING—A municipal ordinance regulating the use that may be made of each parcel of land.

Index